Canoeing Complete

Canoe touring on the Gorge du Tarn, River Tarn, Southern France—
an ideal river for the not so experienced touring canoeist. Spectacular
scenery, a quiet river with some interesting rapids that can be run or
easily portaged, and upwards of five days continuous canoeing make this
river a top favourite among canoe camping canoeists

CANOEING COMPLETE

Edited by Brian Skilling

With contributions by
Alex and Clare Allan, Geoff Blackford, Alan Byde,
Oliver Cock, Chris Hare, Ken Langford,
Jorgen Samson, Geoffrey Sanders, Kathleen Tootill,
Marianne Wilson

Foreword by
John Dudderidge, O.B.E.,
President of the British Canoe Union

53 *line and* 33 *half-tone illustrations*

KAYE & WARD
LONDON

First published by
NICHOLAS KAYE LTD
1966
Revised edition published by
Kaye & Ward Ltd
1973
Second impression 1976

ISBN 0 7182 0938 9

All enquiries and requests relevant to this title should
be sent to the publisher, Kaye & Ward Ltd, 21 New Street,
London EC2M 4NT, and not to the printer.

Printed in England by
Fletcher & Son Ltd, Norwich

Contents

List of Illustrations

PHOTOGRAPHS

PHOTOGRAPHS

DRAWINGS

DRAWINGS

Acknowledgments

The editor would like to thank the following for permission to reproduce the photographs in this book:

Canoeing Press—Jacket; Frontispiece; Nos. 13, 14, 17, 18, 19, 21, 22, 23, 24, 26, 27; Chris Hare—No. 1; J. H. Haward—No. 15; Atlantic College—Nos. 2, 3, 4, 5, 6, 7, 8, 9, 10, 11, 12, 28, 29, 30, 31, 32; E. Lewis—No. 16; Streamlyte—No. 20; E. Boesch—No. 25.

Foreword

IN recent years a good many books on canoeing have appeared' and most of them have made a useful contribution to the literature of the sport. Some have been written for the specialists, some for the novices, and a few have attempted to give a comprehensive picture of what is not one sport but a whole collection of activities, some competitive, some recreational, but all involving the use of a canoe.

With each branch undergoing rapid development it has become increasingly difficult for a single author to write from first hand experience, and this has resulted in parts of his book having the ring of authority and the rest being based on information culled from others. This has been no reflection on the author, for there are few, if any, who today can lay claim to being an authority and expert in every, or even most, branches of the sport.

This book is different, and I have read it with great enjoyment and satisfaction. It does not claim to be encyclopaedic, for every section could be expanded to fill a book, but within the limitations of space it succeeds in conveying a wealth of valuable information and guidance for novice and expert alike. I have known all the contributors for many years and they all write from a wide personal experience as specialists in their subject. The newcomer to canoeing will learn a great deal and will discover the wide variety of canoeing experience open to him, whilst the old hand will be encouraged to improve his skills, and, possibly, to widen his experience in a new direction.

It gives me great pleasure to write this Foreword to a very excellent symposium produced by such a talented group of experts and I congratulate the Editor on his team. I hope the book will be widely read by the ever increasing number of canoeists entering the sport through the schools, outdoor activity centres, youth organisations and the Services.

John Dudderidge

November 1972

Introduction

IN 1865, John MacGregor set out in a canoe of his own design and paddled along a thousand miles of European waterways. This voyage, and his later ones on the Jordan and the Baltic, caught the public imagination, his books describing his adventures became best-sellers, and, perhaps most important of all, he founded a new sport—recreational canoeing.

Over the past hundred years, the sport of canoeing has passed through many phases. MacGregor envisaged the canoe as a small craft which could either be paddled or sailed, and which could provide accommodation afloat if desired, but his contemporaries found the sailing aspect more appealing, and so canoes became larger and heavier, the paddle being used only in an emergency when the wind failed. In the 1880s the introduction of the open Canadian-type canoe from North America brought a temporary revival of interest in paddling, but by the end of the century this had almost vanished except as a casual form of recreation. The sailing canoe continued to enjoy limited popularity, but the cost of these large craft meant that their use was confined to a well-to-do minority.

The twentieth century brought the invention of the collapsible kayak which could easily be transported, and after the First World War canoe touring became immensely popular, especially on the continent. In 1936, canoe paddling races were accepted as an Olympic sport, and paddling was back in favour—and as a pastime well within the reach of most young sportsmen. The expeditions, too, from 1930 to 1933 of Gino Watkins to Greenland; the knowledge and experience which he and other members of his parties gained in kayaking with the Eskimos; and the demonstrations given afterwards in this country of the Eskimo Roll, suggested, almost for the first time to Europeans, the real potential in difficult waters of the expert canoeist in a suitable craft, that (what the Eskimos had known for many years) the canoe hull, the canoeist himself and his paddle must be thought of as one tight-fitting, completely co-ordinated unit.

Although this lesson had not been learnt by the outbreak

of war, and indeed was not really followed up until the 1950s, the canoe proved invaluable for inshore reconnaissance of enemy coastlines, and the raid of Lt-Col Hasler with his 'cockleshell heroes' on the shipping at Bordeaux is one of the most famous of wartime small-craft exploits. After the war, canoeing as a sport continued to grow in popularity, but as more and more people began to own cars, the collapsible kayak gave way to the rigid kayak, often home-built and made of lath-and-canvas, plywood, and latterly of glass-fibre. Increasingly, schools and youth organizations have found in canoeing a pursuit which gives young people an admirable opportunity of developing their creative handicraft talents in canoe construction, and their physical skills in facing the numerous challenges offered by canoeing today.

The past few years have seen a strong growth in specialization, both in the type of craft used and in the skills which have been developed to achieve optimum performance. As a result, whilst the all-rounder can still derive pleasure from the sport practised at his own level, the experts in the various branches are specialists who have devoted themselves to reaching the peak in, for example, slalom, racing or canoe surfing. This is inevitable and good, but one unfortunate side-effect has been that no one person can hope to write with authority and from personal experience on all aspects of the sport. It was with this in mind that the editors conceived the idea of this book: to gather together a group of people who were all experienced leaders in their particular field, and to persuade them to write about it without, however, forgetting the newcomer who needs a more general introduction to the sport. In this way it was hoped to produce a book which could be both comprehensive and to some degree authoritative.

One type of canoe, the Canadian, is, however, mentioned only in the chapter on canoe design. The reason for this is that Canadian canoeing is still a minority activity in this country, and to have included it would have meant either reducing the space devoted to other topics, or increasing the price of the book. It was decided that neither of these courses was justified, not least because the subject has been outstandingly well covered in *Canoeing*, by Joseph L. Hasenfus (published by the American Red Cross), and more briefly in the booklet *Canadian Canoeing* (published by the British Canoe Union.)

We hope with *Canoeing Complete* to impel acceptance of the fact that modern canoeing can no longer be adequately written about by a single author. If we are successful, we shall have set a valuable precedent and perhaps made something of a landmark in canoeing literature. We hope, too, that revised editions of this book may appear from time to time in which current experts will be invited to bring their fellow-canoeists, schools, youth groups, training colleges and the general public up-to-date on the latest developments in their own particular sphere of the sport.

Brian Skilling
David Sutcliffe

INTRODUCTION TO SECOND EDITION

The hopes expressed in the final paragraph of the Introduction to the first edition of *Canoeing Complete* have been fulfilled, and it is my pleasure to introduce this new edition. Much new material has been included in order that the book should continue to represent the best of current thinking on the sport. The editorial policy has remained the same, that is to give each contributor a free hand to select those things which he, or she, feels are important. The result is that not only will readers find the best of advice, but, it is hoped, will catch something of the personalities of the writers.

Brian Skilling

1

Basic Technique

GEOFFREY SANDERS

WHEN practised sensibly, canoeing is a comparatively safe sport. Good instruction in the basic techniques will play an important part in producing a careful and reasonable approach to the sport, because it will enable the beginner to know and appreciate his own limitations and those of the canoes he uses.

To this end it is recommended that where possible the newcomer should either attend a course for beginners or obtain tuition from someone who is qualified to give it. However, material in this chapter is meant for the novice: it is hoped that those able to attend courses will find it useful for preliminary reading or possibly for revision, whilst the beginner who has to teach himself will find it provides a workable basis for self-instruction. For the beginner, especially, there are three preliminary points that must be made.

1. Don't canoe if you are unable to swim.
2. Wear an approved life-jacket and make sure that you know how to put it on correctly.
3. Never go out alone. If it is impossible to get another canoeist to go with you for your first venture afloat, take a sensible friend who can swim. Work out with him beforehand what you will do in the event of a capsize. Study Chapter 8—Oliver Cock on 'Safety in Canoeing'—carefully before you start, checking that the necessary conditions are fulfilled. If your friend has this book with him he might well be able to assist in the instruction by reading out the appropriate commentary.

A. INITIAL TECHNIQUES

For the first practical session we need a nice, easy bank, not more than a foot or two high, and a calm stretch of water. Anything that may produce an unplanned capsize is to be shunned, be it underwater obstacle or overhanging trees. Although trees may look picturesque their branches are only too willing to ensnare the innocent beginner. A capsize will be an essential part of the early instruction—but only when directed! Common sense suggests that the scene of your first introduction into a canoe should be well clear of weirs, rapids, mud flats, and the like, where you could so easily get into difficulties.

Check that you have all your personal gear with you. Apart from your 'travelling' clothes you will need a towel and two sets of canoeing clothes. Make sure that there are some warm garments amongst them—the water may be cold and you will be glad of them after the capsize drill has been practised. Recommended canoeing wear—depending on the weather— includes swimming kit, shorts, vest or singlet ('T' or games type), a sweater or pullover (preferably not a windcheater or track suit as they tend to hold the water and are heavy when wet), anorak or smock. A pair of plastic sandals or cheap gym shoes should be worn on the feet.

1. Carrying the Canoe

Carrying the canoe to the water is a game that one, two, four or six can play! The purpose of the manœuvre is not only that the boat should be transported from point 'A' to point 'B' but also that it should arrive intact. It is probably true that more damage takes place to boats *out* of the water than in the water —simply because they are not handled carefully and correctly. I have seen a canoeist pull a canoe across a field by its painter: another carried the boat on his shoulder but didn't seem to mind that the stern was periodically bouncing off the ground. Good habits for handling canoes out of the water as well as in it should be encouraged from the very beginning.

It is unwise to carry a fully loaded canoe unless there are enough helpers to ensure that it can be carried safely. A loaded double may require as many as four or six people to carry it— one at each end and one or two on each side of the cockpit. An unladened single can be carried with ease by two, with one person holding each end nestled comfortably under his arm. The hand should grasp the keel and rest against the hip. For short portages it is possible to carry the boat on your own. If the distance to be covered is only a few yards, the boat can be held with one arm under the near side of the cockpit with the weight of the boat taken by the hip. Alternatively, the canoe can be carried on the shoulder—the point of balance of the cockpit resting on the shoulder with the elbow and lower arm inside the cockpit to give additional support. Other techniques can be devised later, such as carrying the boat on the head . . . to be watched when there are high winds!

2. Boat Inspection

Before launching the canoe you must always check that your equipment is in order. There must be no loose ends of painters left lying about the cockpit. Seats (and backrests if used) should be firmly attached. Spare clothes, repair kits, etc., should be in waterproof bags and tied into the canoe—making sure that no gear is left cluttering the cockpit where it might obstruct an easy exit in the event of a capsize. (Any heavy equipment should not be placed in the canoe until it is on the water and securely fastened to the bank.) Examine the boat's buoyancy to see that it is adequately attached and inflated. The paddle should be feathered correctly for your own use. (See later under 5). Before putting on your lifejacket, check that it is in sound order and make sure that you adjust it correctly.

3. Launching

Care is needed in launching as well as carrying the boat. It is not enough to slide it into the water: there may be sharp stones or broken pieces of glass waiting to scratch if not tear the hull. The canoe must never be moved whilst it is in contact with the ground: if this simple rule is kept, there are many ways in which the craft can be safely launched and removed from the water.

(a) *Two-man launch:* one at each side of the cockpit. Holding the boat at 90 degrees to the bank, the stern is lowered into the water and the rest of the canoe then 'handed down', keeping it as low as possible to the bank without actually touching. The bow is then manœuvred round so that it is facing upstream (or against the wind) and the boat is parallel to the bank.

(b) *Single-man launch:* the canoe held at 90 degrees to the bank either against the knees, with both hands holding the edge of the cockpit, or on the hip, with a supporting arm in the cockpit. The stern is lowered into the water as in the two-man launch and pulled round until it is adjacent to the bank.

Variations on these methods are possible and often necessary where the launching site is awkward. A modification of the single-man launch, for example, is to hold the canoe across the thighs and to place it in the water parallel to the side. One hand holds the boat by the cockpit, the other the gunwale to prevent it from chafing the bank. If the boat is at all heavy, this method often requires more strength than a youngster possesses. A failure to calculate accurately the distance to the edge of the bank can also result in the launching of the canoeist as well as the canoe!

4. Embarkation

Before very long you will be entering your boat in many different ways as required by the situation of the moment and you will have forgotten your first uncertain seconds when trying to master the art. For a canoe, rather like a bicycle, needs to be approached with care. Once you have mastered the basic essentials, you can venture forth and experiment with new methods. In the initial instruction, therefore, perfect two methods of entry into the canoe—one from the land and the other from shallow water. Entry from overhanging trees and other applied gymnastic feats can be left until later!

There are two important things to remember:

(*a*) Until you are really competent, do everything *slowly* and deliberately.

(*b*) Where possible all parts of the anatomy should be kept *central* when coming into contact with the boat.

And now for the operation itself.

FROM THE BANK

(i) *Embarkation*

Let us imagine that you are standing on the bank, facing the bow of the boat which is in the water alongside and to your right.

(*a*) Kneel or crouch—with the cockpit of the canoe to your right.

(*b*) LEFT hand; clutching a clump of grass or flat on the ground. Keep it in this position until you are comfortably seated in the canoe—it will ensure your equilibrium, of mind as well as body!

RIGHT hand—to the front of the cockpit (or as near as you can reach it on the right-hand side if the cockpit is a long one).

Fig. 1 Embarkation from a bank

(*c*) RIGHT leg into the centre of the boat, leaving sufficient room between it and the seat for your other foot.

(*d*) LEFT hand remains on bank.
LEFT foot into canoe, behind right.

(*e*) LEFT hand remains on bank.
RIGHT hand on front of cockpit.
SLOWLY lower yourself into the seat.

(*f*) Make yourself comfortable. If you need to change your seating position remember that any movement must be a balanced movement. If your hands are to take your weight put them behind you—say, one on either side of the back of the cockpit. Remember that being comfortable in a canoe really means being a part of the canoe. Your feet should be against the footrest (you may have to disembark to adjust it); your knees pressed against the side of the underside of the cockpit (depending on the boat) and your seat secure, preferably with hip supports. A loose or wobbly seat is a possible source of danger and a hard, moulded seat, besides being better from the canoeing and safety points of view, is usually much more comfortable on a long journey.

Before disembarking test the *stability* of the boat . . . and yourself! Push off a little from the side, raise your hands above your head and rock the boat from side to side. Bend sideways from the hips to left and right and you will find that you can rock the boat to left and right with your knees and seat—provided that they are sufficiently well anchored in the boat.

Fig. 2   Embarkation from shallow water

Can you get water lapping into the cockpit without capsizing the canoe?

(ii) *Disembarkation*

Follow the reverse procedure to embarkation:

(*a*) LEFT hand to hold bank.

(*b*) Bring knees close up to body. RIGHT hand to front of cockpit.

(*c*) Feet still in the boat. Raise body until standing. LEFT hand still on the bank: RIGHT on front of the cockpit.

(*d*) LEFT foot out, followed by RIGHT.

FROM SHALLOW WATER

(i) *Embarkation*

There will be many occasions on shallow rivers where you will have to enter your boat from water up to knee depth. In a normal touring boat the procedure is as follows:

You are standing in the water by your boat, with the cockpit to your right.

(*a*) Place your RIGHT leg in the cockpit. (Shake mud, water etc. from the foot first.)

(*b*) Place both hands behind the body—position them one either side of the cockpit behind the seat.

(c) Take the weight of your body on the hands and, thus balanced, bring your left leg into the canoe. (Again, shake the foot dry if time allows.) Lower yourself into a comfortable sitting position.

(ii) *Disembarkation*

(a) Hands are placed behind the body on the back of the cockpit.

(b) Weight of the body taken by the hands.

(d) Left leg out—takes the weight of the body—hands can be moved, right one to front of cockpit—right leg follows.

In a canoe with a very small cockpit this method may not be practicable, as there will not be sufficient room to push the knees below the deck. Beginners with this kind of boat are advised to delay attempting embarkation from shallow water until they are really familiar with the boat. They will then be able to devise methods of entry—for example, using a modified 'bank' entry with the paddle serving as an outrigger.

Practise such methods of embarkation and disembarkation until you can do them without thinking.

Now pull the canoe out of the water and we can introduce you to the paddle!

5. Paddling Strokes

HOLDING THE PADDLE

You can practise holding the paddle on dry land for a few moments to check that you grasp it in the correct fashion and have the right idea as far as the stroke is concerned. Many beginners have their wrists much too close together on the paddle. Support the paddle on your head with your elbows at right angles—this will give you about the right grip.

Use the blades feathered—that is, at right angles to each other—from the start. This makes for easier paddling in the long run. One hand is going to hold the paddle firmly; the wrist will, therefore, be doing a lot of the work when it twists the shaft of the paddle through the necessary 90 degrees. The shaft of the paddle is going to swivel through the other wrist and so obviously the grasp will not be such a tight one. Try this for yourself and watch the movement of the blades. Thumbs are under the shaft, by the way. Decide which wrist you prefer to do the work and, if the paddles are spooned, adjust them accordingly. Try a few 'fresh air' strokes and if all seems well you are ready for the water!

FORWARD PADDLING

Once you are afloat push away from the bank—with your hand and not the paddle. Check that your grip is correct in relation to the paddle blades. The stroke is a natural one, but there are three points that should be remembered. It should be a *LONG* stroke. Push one arm forward until it is straight in front and even then push it a little further by turning the shoulders. Don't let your wrist cross the centre line of the boat. Your other arm will, of course, be pulling back the other blade through the water until your wrist is more or less in line with the body and near the cockpit coaming. It is also a

LOW stroke. For normal cruising your pushing hand will go down towards the front of the cockpit rather than up towards the head. The paddle blades need not go much above your head. Furthermore let your first movements be

SLOW and deliberate. Don't rush them: work out each stroke carefully in your mind, especially as far as the feathering movement is concerned. Watch the blade in the water until you are sure that you automatically start the stroke correctly. At the point of entry the blade will be at an angle of about 45 degrees to the surface of the water, but after the initial few inches it will be at right angles—excepting again the last few inches of the stroke. See that only the blade and not the shaft of the paddle is immersed during the stroke.

PRACTISE until you find that you don't need to watch the blade each time that it enters the water . . . and then don't. There is nothing that looks quite so ungainly as the canoeist who turns his head every time he makes a stroke.

BACKWARD PADDLING

It is simply the reverse of forward paddling and as such does not require careful enumeration here. You make the stroke with the back of the blade and even if the blade is spooned you do not turn them. Watch the first few strokes to check on the correct angle of entry of the blade into the water. Remember . . . long . . . low . . . slow strokes!

STOPPING

There are no brakes in a canoe and it is impracticable to carry an anchor to throw out when you want to stop! Push the vertical paddle into the water, level with your body—first on one side and then on the other. If necessary, add a short backward stroke on each occasion. Be ready for the sudden braking, especially when travelling at a fair speed, by bracing yourself in the canoe.

TURNING

Turning will soon come naturally but it is useful in the early stages of instruction to practise deliberately the different turning methods. As in driving a car, always try to anticipate your moves well beforehand.

Right turn: an extra forward stroke on the left and/or a backward stroke on the right.

Left turn: an extra stroke on the right and/or a backward stroke on the left. (See also 'Sweep stroke' p. 30.)

FERRY GLIDE

A manœuvre which will enable you to put into practice some of the strokes you have already learnt, and which is to be considered essential for river canoeing, can now be introduced. Called the 'Ferry Glide', it enables the canoe to glide across the stream when it is desired to alter the course of the boat after some obstacle has been sighted ahead. It represents a way of using the power of the stream to move the boat sideways and can be used when proceeding upstream or downstream.

(i) *Downstream.* As soon as you see the obstacle:

(*a*) Effect one strong backward paddle stroke on the side you *don't* want to go. This will have the effect of slightly turning the bow of the boat at an angle to the current in the direction you *don't* want to go.

(*b*) Back paddle on the same side again and then on both sides alternately. The stream will carry the canoe across the stream in the desired direction. Continue back paddling until you see the clear passage ahead.

(ii) *Upstream.* As soon as you see that you have to change your course:

(*a*) Execute one strong forward paddle stroke on the side that you *don't* want to go. This will turn the bow in the direction that you *do want* to go.

(*b*) Give another forward stroke on the same side and then on both sides alternately. Continue forward paddling until you are far enough across the stream.

The strength of the current will determine the angle of the boat to the main stream, but beware at all costs of putting the boat broadside against the current. Quite a slight angle, say of 10

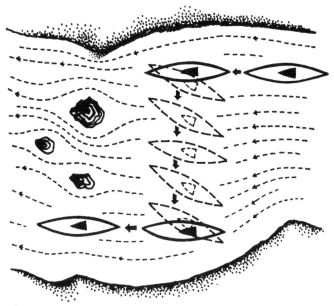

Fig. 3 Ferry Glide (facing downstream). The angle of the canoe is varied according to the speed of the current

degrees, will often suffice and experience will soon enable you to judge the right amount of strength to put into that initial stroke. It is a sound plan to practise ferry glides on every new piece of moving water that you attempt. You can even try out the initial emergency strokes on still water to show that you have got the right reaction. Many people have been taught the manœuvre on canals and have been able to apply what they have learnt on their first river trip.

PULLING INTO THE BANK

Here the paddle blade can be used as a rudder in order to turn the boat parallel to the bank. Experiment well away from the bank in the first instance. Push the paddle out just to the rear of your body with the blade, vertical in the water, at about 45 degrees to the boat. You may find it helpful to hold the shaft of the paddle against the side of the boat. If the canoe is moving when you make this 'stern rudder' stroke, it will have the effect of turning the bow towards the paddle side. Head the canoe towards the bank at an angle of about 45 degrees. Remember that you will want to land with the bow pointing upstream, or into the wind. As you approach the bank apply the 'stern rudder' on the opposite side of the boat to the bank. Practice will make perfect but, until it does so, avoid shortening the canoe by trying to widen the bank!

TWO-SEATER TECHNIQUES

I have assumed that the beginner is going to use a single-seater canoe. Even if he possesses a double there is much to be said in favour of his using it as a single for the initial stages of instruction. When it comes to be used by two people, there are additional factors that must be considered.

The stern man is the captain and is responsible for the control of the boat.

The bow man sets the stroke—long, low and slow to start with—and continues with this unless the captain orders otherwise. The bow man is in a much better position to see obstacles and he should pass the word back to the captain if he sights any; but the stern man is much better placed to take evasive action. The bow man can often continue with the normal paddling rhythm whilst the stern man, say, misses a stroke on one side or even applies a 'stern rudder' stroke. The bow man may be asked to apply a forward sweep stroke (described later on p. 30) whilst the stern man uses a backward sweep. Paddling must be synchronized—the paddles in unison and not simulating a windmill! The clashes (and cracks?) that the latter style will inevitably cause will not lead to harmony between the paddlers either! The more practice the pair can get together, the more effective will be the paddling.

This should provide sufficient instruction for your first session on the water. The important thing now is to try all these out for yourself and to become really familiar with the different skills. A short trip on calm waters can be recommended as it will enable you to become really familiar with the boat. Keep trying the turns in as many varied situations as you can find. Improvise a simple 'still water' slalom course where you can paddle round obstacles, paying more attention to style than speed at this stage.

If it is possible, I would strongly recommend that you practise a deliberate capsize at one stage during this first session afloat. It is an important safety drill and will also give you considerable confidence. You will learn to appreciate that a capsize is in no way to be feared in normal circumstances. The drill is explained by Oliver Cock in Chapter 8.

B. PROFICIENCY SKILLS

Instruction should not cease once you are able to paddle around, even if with a fair degree of competence. Although many who consider themselves to be proficient canoeists go no further than this, it is now generally recognized that further instruction is extremely valuable and is to be wholeheartedly encouraged. The canoeist himself will obtain greater enjoyment and gain new confidence from being able to exercise much greater control over his boat. This will stand him in good stead when he has to face difficult waters and hazards, and will give him a clearer insight into the capacities of the boat and his ability to handle it.

Two Preliminary Points

Before describing the different strokes, I should like you to note the following:

(*a*) The *hand position* on the paddles should remain as for normal paddling: the hands should not be moved into a positon that appears better for the particular stroke being attempted. Half the point of these basic strokes is that they can be used at any time—quickly—from the normal paddling position. If the paddles to be used for instruction are too long, it may be necessary to experiment with change of hand positions in order to get the feel of the stroke. If this is the case, obtain a shorter pair as soon as you can.

(*b*) You should now begin to try controlled '*leans*' in your canoe. As you paddle in a forward direction—without interrupting the continuity of the paddling and with your hips and lower body braced in the canoe—lean the boat to one side, keeping your trunk as upright as possible. Most canoes have a tendency to turn away from the lean. Experiment with the effects of leans—of both boat and body—in the different strokes. In the case of forward paddling, for example, you will have discovered a means of turning the boat without breaking the rhythm of paddling.

Sweep Strokes

The sweep stroke is a means of turning the boat more quickly, and is really an exaggerated turn stroke (described earlier). It can be used when the canoe is stationary or moving slowly. To turn the canoe a complete circle one keeps using a long forward stroke (forward sweep) on one side and a long backward stroke (backward sweep) on the opposite side. For example, to turn the boat to the right or in a clockwise direction, lean and reach forward, letting the left blade enter the water vertically as near the bow as possible. Bring this blade round in a full arc until it is near the stern of the boat, by which time you should be leaning slightly backwards and towards the blade. Then turn the body to place the right blade in the water near the stern and bring it forwards in a wide circle to the bow.

Practise . . . first one way and then the other. How many strokes are required to turn the boat through 360 degrees? Can you improve on this by leaning a little further?

Fig. 4   Sweep stroke

Two Recovery Strokes

A canoeist will often be faced by situations when his balance is threatened. An unseen boulder may jar the hull of his canoe or an unexpected wave cause him to lurch perilously. The competent paddler will be able to remedy this at once by the quick application of a recovery stroke—using the paddle to push himself back into a position which enables him to resume full control of the boat.

RECOVERY BY SLAP SUPPORT

(1) *Starting position:* Brace yourself in the cockpit, leaning slightly forwards. Normal paddle grip. Paddle at right angles to the boat, just in front of the body. Blade just above and parallel to the water. Concave side upwards if using a curved blade.

(2) *Action:* Lean towards the blade and press firmly and sharply on the paddle to bring yourself to the vertical position again.

    Note:—Paddle at right angles to the boat.

            Blade flat on the water.

            A firm, quick push.

(3) *Practice:* Tip the boat a little further each time until water is lapping round and into the cockpit. Try it on each side and, when you have got the knack of twisting the paddle to ensure that the blades are flat to the water, try a series of recovery strokes on alternate sides. When you feel really competent, ask someone to hold the stern of the boat and rock it unexpectedly to the left and right: see if you can prevent him from turning you out!

Fig. 5   Sculling for support

SCULLING FOR SUPPORT

(1) *Starting position:* Brace yourself in the cockpit, leaning slightly forwards. Normal paddle grip. Paddle pointing forwards at about 45 degrees to the boat. Paddle nearly flat on the water, the edge towards the stern of the boat being raised slightly (some 10 degrees). Concave side upwards if using a curved blade.

(2) *Action:* The paddle is going to be swept round in an arc for approximately 90 degrees. It will then be pointing towards the stern, at about 45 degrees to the boat. The edge of the blade that is 'leading the way' must always be slightly raised. Thus on the return stroke the other edge of the blade (i.e., the edge facing the bow) must be raised. The paddle is then kept moving continuously, the leading edge always being raised. If you have difficulty in knowing which way to twist the blade, remember that the same side of the paddle must always face the boat.

Try this slowly along the surface of the water, experimenting with the angle of the blade to the water, and turning the blade at the beginning and end of the arc. When you can do this without looking at the paddle, lean towards the blade in the water . . . further . . . and further . . . until the cockpit is awash. The blade will support you so long as you keep it moving and at the right angle to the water.

(3) *Practice:* Practise on both sides, seeing how far you can go! If you find yourself going too far and are in danger of capsizing, apply a quick recovery stroke by slap support in order to right yourself. A good canoeist will use one or other of these strokes, or a combination of both, to right himself in difficult moments. Imagine that you hit a submerged boulder at different moments of the normal paddling stroke and react accordingly. Ideally, practise these strokes at a time when a capsize is not too uncomfortable—a session in an indoor swimming pool in the winter can be very useful. If the thought of a capsize does not worry you, you will perfect these strokes much more quickly.

Two Sideways or Draw Strokes

It is desirable to be able to manœuvre the canoe into any required position. Draw strokes, therefore, should be mastered by the beginner who is anxious to feel that he is in full control of his boat. There will be many occasions, not only in slalom competitions but also in general touring, when he will find it useful to be able to move the boat in a sideways direction.

DRAW STROKE

(1) *Starting position:* Brace yourself in the cockpit, leaning slightly forwards. Normal paddle grip. Paddle at right angles to the boat. Stretch the paddle over to one side—the blade near the water, parallel to and as far away from the boat as can be reached comfortably. Concave side of blade towards the canoe.

(2) *Action:* (*a*) Draw the paddle, blade fully covered, into the side of the boat. STOP when the blade is near (not touching) the boat and the paddle is vertical: to proceed further than this point will demonstrate how a paddle can lever you out of a canoe!

(*b*) Twist the blade through an angle of 90 degrees and slice it through the water back to the starting position. (Alternatively, the blade can be sliced out of the water, without

Fig. 6　Draw stroke

turning, towards the stern of the canoe and then carried through the air to the starting position. This method of recovery tends to be slower, however, and is not quite so neat).

(*c*) Having got the 'feel' of the stroke, lean towards the paddle—this will make the draw much more effective. Return to the vertical position just before the end of the actual draw stroke.

(3) *Practice:* Practise on both sides of the canoe, across the river or canal. If there are two canoes present, have a sideways race! Try the effect of the draw stroke not just with the paddle at 90 degrees to the boat but placed at different angles, both towards the bow and stern. Don't be satisfied until you can really lean into your stroke. The timing of this, of course, requires plenty of practice.

SCULLING DRAW

(1) *Starting position:* The beginner is advised to approach the sculling draw from the sculling-for-support stroke. Start with the paddle travelling in its arc to and fro along the surface of the water. There is no need to lean out on the paddle on this occasion as the stroke is not going to be used for support.

(2) *Action:* Continuing the movement of the stroke bring the blade in towards the side of the canoe—the blade out of the

Fig. 7   Sculling draw

water will thus move to a position where it is nearly vertical above the blade in the water. Keep the blade moving—it will be following the shape of a figure eight and will be moving the boat sideways towards the paddle. If this does not quite work out first time, go back to the sculling-for-support movement and try again. Examine the parts of the sculling draw stroke. Note how the leading edge of the blade is pointing away from the boat all the time. In order to achieve this, the angle of the paddle has to be changed continually. Experiment with different angles.

(*If you have the leading edge of the blade pointing towards the boat instead of away from it, this will have the effect of pushing the boat away from the paddle and will move you in a direction away from the paddle side. This stroke is not recommended for general use as it is rather an awkward one to perform. Try it by all means—when the water is warm! As a general rule it is better to perfect draw and sculling draw strokes for both sides of the boat.*)

If you are using a spooned blade, try the concave side facing the boat—it should make the stroke more effective.

(3) *Practice:* Practise the stroke on the opposite side when you can do it well on your 'first' side. Lean out to the stroke: as in the case of the other sideways stroke, it will enable you to reach out further from the boat with the paddle, thus making each stroke more effective and helping the boat in its sideways movement.

Try the sculling draw in different positions in relation to the canoe. In how many directions can you propel the canoe by the use of this stroke? Practise 'emergency situations' where you might have to move the boat sideways in a hurry. Placing of obstacles on still water or the erection of a slalom gate will give you good scope for testing the degree of your proficiency. Note how you can often use a combination of both sideways strokes—draw and sculling draw—to gain the desired movement. Try the 'Wiggle Test'—outlined in Chapter 11.

When you feel proficient in the handling of your canoe you will really begin to feel a part of the boat. You will enjoy feeling it respond to every movement and stroke. The BCU Proficiency Test (see Appendix I) is designed to assess your capabilities, and candidates are required to perform all the skills described in this chapter. Even if you don't feel like actually taking the test, it provides a useful guide to the standard that you should be striving to achieve.

The BCU Advanced Tests are for the experienced canoeist who is competent to demonstrate the more advanced strokes, including the Eskimo Roll. Although it is beyond the scope of this chapter to explain the Advanced strokes it is perhaps worth mentioning, however, that they are simply an extension or mixture of one or more of the basic strokes that have been considered. 'High' strokes, for example, are an adaptation of the basic strokes with the paddle held over the head: a Telemark turn combines backward sweep and sculling for support strokes. If the basic strokes are well and truly mastered— and this means practising them to the stage where they come automatically according to the needs of the moment—the canoeist can proceed to study the more advanced strokes with confidence. He is even likely to improvise his own and, indeed, there is a great deal of pleasure to be gained from devising the best possible means of keeping full control over the boat in all kinds of water.

2

The Eskimo Roll

GEOFF BLACKFORD

THE most extraordinary feat of kayak handling is the ability to right the craft after a capsize whilst remaining in the canoe. This manœuvre is called 'Rolling'. I teach students to roll in about thirty minutes; they can then go away and canoe. Two very different statements, and somewhere between these two points of view, is the right perspective. In this chapter it is not my intention to say that any one approach is right or wrong, but rather to show differing systems of rolling and methods of teaching, tell something of their history and development, and then leave it to the reader to decide for himself which is the right method for him in any given situation.

The art of kayak rolling was developed to a high degree in Alaska and Greenland where it was a matter of survival for the Eskimo in the event of a capsize while seal hunting or fishing. There is little recorded information about the Alaskan kayakers, but ethnographers and explorers have made a fairly extensive study of the Greenlanders. The earliest detailed record is that of David Crantz, a European missionary, who in 1767 in his *History of Greenland* enumerated ten methods of rolling. His description was as follows:

'1. The Greenlander lays himself first on one side, then on the other, with his body flat upon the water (to imitate the case of one who is nearly, but not quite overset) and keeps the balance with his pautik or oar, so that he raises himself again.

'2. He overturns himself quite, so that his head hangs perpendicular underwater; in this dreadful posture he gives himself a swing with a stroke of his paddle, and raises himself aloft again on which side he will.

'These are the most common cases of misfortune, which frequently occur in storms and high waves; but they still suppose that the Greenlander retains the advantage of his pautik in his hand, and is disentangled from the seal-leather strap. But it may easily happen in the seal-fishery, that the man becomes entangled with the string, so that he cannot rightly use the pautik, or that he loses it entirely. Therefore they must be prepared for this casualty. With this in view

'3. They run one end of the pautik under one of the cross-strings of the kajak, (to imitate its being entangled) overset, and scrabble up again by means of the artful motion of the other end of the pautik.

'4. They hold one end of it in their mouth, and yet move the other end with their hand, so as to rear themselves upright again.

'5. They lay the pautik behind their neck, and hold it there with both hands, or,

'6. Hold it fast behind their back; so overturn, and by stirring it with both their hands behind them, without bringing it before, rise and recover,

'7. They lay it across one shoulder, take hold of it with one hand before, and the other hand behind their back, and thus emerge from the deep.

'These exercises are of service in cases where the pautik is entangled with string; but because they may also quite lose it, in which the greatest danger lies, therefore,

'8. Another exercise is to run the pautik through the water under the kajak, hold it fast on both sides with their face lying on the kajak, in this position overturn, and rise again by moving the oar *secundum artem* on the top of the water from beneath. This is of service when they lose the oar during over-setting, and yet see it swimming over them, to learn to manage it with both hands from below.

'9. They let the oar go, turn themselves head down, reach their hand after it, and from the surface pull it down to them, and so rebound up.

'10. But if they can't possibly reach it, they take either the hand-board off from the harpoon, or a knife, and try by force of these, or even splashing the water with the palm of their hand, to swing themselves above the water; but this seldom succeeds.'

Since Crantz's time more than thirty methods of rolling have been known in Greenland. There are possibly many more but a precise figure is difficult to arrive at because some are variations and others combinations of basic rolls.

John (Rob Roy) MacGregor popularised the sport of recreational canoeing in the mid-nineteenth century, but it wasn't until the 1920's that the value of rolling began to be appreciated by the sporting canoeist. But even after the 1939–1945 war there were comparatively few exponents of the art, and it was only in the late 1940's when a slalomist first rolled in a competition that the modern enthusiasm for rolling developed.

Rolling was encouraged for the slalomist by having an 'Artificial Natural Hazard' which was a beam suspended low over the water under which the canoeist had to pass without touching to remain penalty free. It was not very long, however, before a lean to surface level and a good recovery stroke was found to be equally effective and a considerable time saver and therefore the 'Artificial Natural Hazard' was dropped. But in the meantime, methods of rolling had evolved to such a degree that in the event of an unintentional capsize most of the top paddlers were able to right themselves.

1. Preparing to hunt for seal in the Rink Fjord, N.W. Greenland.
   Chris Hare farthest from the camera

The recreational sea canoeist tended to be a little more reluctant to attempt rolling in the early days because if the roll was not successful he was in a very different predicament to the river canoeist—the shore may be miles away and that could be serious. Sea rolling began to develop when many of the top international slalomists started to go to the north coast of Cornwall to gain experience of big, heavy waves, of the type seldom found on British rivers. In practising their slalom and white water skills in the surf, they demonstrated the value and art of sea rolling—something the Eskimo had always known.

During the late 1950's the British Canoe Union Coaching Scheme was being evolved, and was officially recognised by the Ministry of Education in 1961. With the formation of the scheme, coaches and instructors began to think about their methods of teaching, and the theories and the practice of canoe rolling were studied along with other aspects of the sport. It is interesting to note that in the beginning there were two main categories of coach/instructor. Firstly, there was the canoeist who was a fine exponent of the sport and who wanted to involve others so that they might gain similar enjoyment to that which he had experienced. On the other hand, there was the teacher who saw the obvious educational possibilities of a sport such as canoeing, and who had the teaching technique but not the canoeing skills. As the Coaching Scheme has reached maturity this gap has narrowed until it is now almost impossible to differentiate between the two groups.

Many schools have swimming pools and, although they are perhaps unable to get on to reasonable canoeing water during their normal school time-table, are able to use canoes in these pools. Here lies an ideal situation for the teaching of rolling and of the basic strokes, although it must be remembered that paddling forwards and backwards with a good technique is difficult in restricted areas. Swimming pool rolling is an ideal teaching situation, but as soon as the skill is learnt it must be practised in the place where it is going to be put to use, in the sea or on a rapid river. If baths rolling is the ultimate, then we are only producing circus performers, and those of not a very high standard.

In the earliest days of rolling, the approach to teaching was very much a matter of trial and error. The instructor would say, 'This is how it's done', do a quick roll, and then tell the student to go away and practise. There was no break-down of the skill.

The result was that it was generally assumed that the art of rolling was to put the paddle into the correct position and lever oneself to the surface. There was little thought of body position, and the usual teaching sequence was the 'Put Across', followed by the 'Pawlata', and then the 'Screw'.

THE PUT ACROSS ROLL

There are several different approach methods to the Put Across Roll, but basically the paddle is slipped out to one side and at right angles to the keel line of the perpendicular upside-down canoe, the paddler then reaches for the surface with the extended blade which is horizontal and pulls up towards the surface.

One method of achieving this is to sit in the upright position, extend the paddle out to one side, placing the extended blade flat on the surface of the water. The arms should be comfortably apart with one hand holding the loom, or shaft, and the other gripping the end of the blade. Capsize towards the extended paddle, without altering the hand grip. Keep the arms relaxed so that when the canoe reaches the upside-down position, the arms are 'wound-up' and the extended paddle has remained on the surface. All that then has to be done to right the canoe is to unwind the arms.

Another approach to the 'wind-up' for the Put Across Roll is as follows: with the canoe in the upright position place the paddle at right angles across the deck with the left-hand paddle blade perpendicular to the surface of the water. The hands should be in the normal paddling grip. Capsize to the left. When completely upside down, slide the paddle out to the left (all the directions are given as the paddler would see them if he were the right way up), cross the right hand over the left so that the right-hand knuckles are facing aft. Take the left forearm under the shaft and the right hand blade, and grasp the end with the left-hand knuckles facing forwards, thus turning the left-hand, or extended, blade into the horizontal position. The paddle is then in the 'wound-up' position, and all that remains to be done is the unwind to bring the paddler upright and so complete the Put Across Roll. All this sounds fairly complicated, but a practice in the swimming pool with a companion standing by will soon clarify any obscure points.

The advantage of this method of rolling is that the paddle is fully extended and provides the maximum leverage possible. The disadvantages are; that both hands have to be removed from the paddle at some time during the roll and therefore there is a geater chance of losing it, particularly in rough water conditions; the large amount of time spent under water on a rapid river increases the possibility of harm to the paddler from passing rocks; the need to place the paddle at right angles to the keel line of the canoe requires considerable expertise in rapidly moving water. Because of these things, the pure Put Across method of rolling has largely been discarded, although some parts have been retained and are used in more recently evolved techniques.

THE PAWLATA ROLL

The Pawlata method of rolling was first performed in Europe by an Austrian, Herr Pawlata, and has for a long time been accepted as a standard teaching roll. This method of rolling is not an end in itself but leads on to the Screw and Storm Rolls. A method of teaching the Pawlata Roll is:

The student must be made to feel at home both in his canoe and in the water—whether the right way up or not. This is best achieved by a gradual build-up in progressive stages to the complete roll. The student must first get into his canoe, making sure that it fits comfortably, and, if not, make appropriate adjustments. Next, he paddles round to get the feeling of the canoe and the paddle, returning to the instructor who should be standing in the water. In his own time, the student capsizes and makes a controlled escape. This is best done by leaning forwards and pushing down on the cockpit coaming (see Chapter 8—Capsize Drill). After the canoe has been emptied and the paddler is on board once more, the canoe is capsized again but this time the student should remain in the canoe and when upside down should lean to one side, look for the surface, and dog-paddle to the edge of the swimming pool, pulling himself up on the bar (plates 2, 3). This manœuvre should be performed with the spray cover in position. The exercise should be practised until it can be performed with confidence, and as experience is gained the student should be encouraged to capsize, hang upside down for as long as he feels fit, and then remove the spray cover, escaping with a forward somersault.

The next stage is for the student to hold the gunwale on the

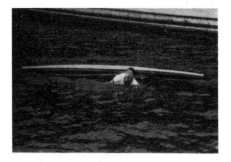

2. Swimming in the canoe and coming up for air

3. A confidence-building exercise, also used with an underhand grip

side towards which he is going to capsize and to twist his body in the same direction. With both hands on the gunwale he will become used to this position by the time he eventually is given the paddle. He then capsizes and the instructor takes him by the hands and pulls him to the surface. As confidence is gained, the student is given more time to look around, and eventually will pull himself up with no effort on the part of the instructor. at this stage the paddle is introduced. The paddle is held with the blade extended on one side and flat on the surface of the water, and at right angles to the keel line. One hand is held on the end of the inboard blade and the other on the shaft, the hands being a comfortable distance apart. The canoe is tipped slightly towards the extended blade and is righted by pushing the shaft towards the water—the inboard hand acting as a fulcrum. After reasonable practice the student should be able to lean over to the point where his shoulder is in the water and be able to right the canoe every time. From this stage it is not a very big step to going completely upside down and righting, which is virtually the Put Across Roll.

Later the paddle is taken in a forward direction as the canoe is capsized. The blade must still remain on the surface, and the righting movement is achieved by sweeping the blade rearwards with the leading edge upwards at a sufficient angle to support the canoeist. This operation is done gently to start with, and the forward sweep increased as the lean and confidence are built up until the upside down position is reached and the paddle starts parallel with the gunwale.

When the student is able to go down and come up on the same side, and has done it many times, he may then try capsizing on the opposite side with the paddle pressed hard against the gunwale towards which he is capsizing and the forward blade flat on the bow deck. After a pause underwater he then comes up on the side that he has practised. Assuming that all this practice has been done in the swimming pool, the student must now go and develop his newly acquired skills in the situation where he will normally be canoeing. When he can roll up in the event of an accidental capsize on either side in cold, rough water, he is well on the way to full confidence.

This system of teaching is flexible and may be lengthened or shortened at any stage to suit any particular student, but it is important that confidence is reached at all stages before proceeding to the next stage.

The traditional pattern of instruction is sound as far as it goes, but often only achieves a partial success rate. Many students struggle up by using a great deal of energy, and when they become tired they just struggle. With the use of swimming baths becoming more common and physical education teachers introducing an analytical approach, the present day teaching method has evolved. As with the earlier methods, confidence building is still of utmost importance and therefore capsizing and getting out without panic, capsizing and looking around, capsizing and dog-paddling to the edge of the bath, or to the instructor, are still essential build-up exercises.

Up until this time, concentration has been on getting the body upright by levering or pulling up on the paddle blade. With the new look it is far more important to get the canoe as upright as possible while the weight of the head and body is supported by the water. The amount of lean that a paddler can achieve without the canoe capsizing always amazes the beginner. It is, therefore, advantageous to use this basic stability in helping to right the canoe when rolling.

It is of the utmost importance to convince the student of the need to get the canoe upright first, and to worry about getting his head and body upright afterwards. This is, perhaps, best achieved by sitting the student in his canoe near the edge of the swimming pool. He then holds the bar with both hands in an underhand grip, palms facing skyward; this will make a brute force pull up more difficult. Holding on to the bar he capsizes towards the edge of the bath, allowing the canoe to go completely upside down on top of him. Let the student try to get up with his head and shoulders first, and in most cases he will only pull himself out of the canoe. Next, he is told to raise the canoe upright by a body twisting movement known as the 'Hip Flick', or hip rotation. This is helped by pushing the leg on the opposite side to the hands (when in the upright position) straight out exerting pressure on the footrest, and at the same time lifting the other knee firmly on to the underside of the deck or kneegrip. If at first the student meets with little success, a gentle hand on the head to hold him underwater until the canoe is nearly upright works wonders. Once success is achieved, only a few repetitions should be done as the bar can give a false sense of security.

The student is now given a polystyrene swimming float on which to attempt recovery, and to give confidence the instructor should stand in the water, slightly behind the student. In the event of failure, the instructor puts his arm under the armpit of his student and lifts him towards the surface so that he can get air and listen to what is being said. It may well be that the student is trying to bring his body from the water at right angles to the canoe. If he can lower his centre of gravity this will greatly assist in righting. There are two methods of lowering the centre of gravity. The first is by bending forward and trying to touch the head on to the knees but many people are not sufficiently flexible to achieve this, and second, by leaning back so that the head is as near as possible touching the stern deck. This latter method is made easier in many modern canoes because of the forward positioning of the seat within the cockpit.

In the event of there being no swimming float available, a life jacket may be used, but the student must be made to understand that this is only a training method and that he must under no circumstances remove his life jacket in other capsizing situations for a similar use.

If the instructor prefers, he may give the student a paddle shaft in the horizontal position from which to recover. This has the advantage that the instructor can feel the amount of effort the student is using to right himself. In the early stages, the student will exert a great deal of strength, but as time progresses less effort will be needed, and the smaller the effort the nearer the student is to rolling.

Once the student has complete confidence in his ability to right himself using a swimming float, or paddle, for support, he can be taught one of the basic methods of rolling. Most people at this stage are taught an adaptation of the Pawlata method. The Pawlata method is to place the paddle on the fore deck in the extended position. The canoe is capsized and the paddle is swept in as large an arc as possible along the surface of the water three-quarters of the way towards the stern and returned to about right angles to the keel line, whilst the paddler is righting himself.

4, 5 & 6. The Pawlata roll

Many of the modern rollers are in the upright position by the time the paddle reaches the right angle on the backward sweep and if not they will finish recovery with what is virtually the last part of the Put Across Roll. This is not a true Pawlata since the supporting sculling action has not been completed. Such a stroke could perhaps be called the Pawlata Across, for if we are going to use the original name we should make sure that the roll is performed in the way that it was originally.

THE STEYR ROLL

Very often when running a large surf wave, or on a rapid river, the canoeist together with his paddle is knocked along the stern deck by the sheer force of water. In these circumstances it is unwise to attempt to put the paddle into the start position along the bow deck, particularly as the rear paddle position is suited to the start of another roll, the Steyr.

The Steyr Roll has one advantage over most of the other methods of rolling in as much as it can be taught on dry land, and in fact without either canoe or paddle—an ordinary household broom will suffice. The student sits on the floor with his legs outstretched. He is given a broom to hold by the handle with the head extended to one side. The handle is held with the knuckles upwards, as though it were an ordinary paddle. The hand furthest from the broom head is the fulcrum, and the other is the lever hand. The student is then told to fall towards the broom head and as he does so, to straighten his body by leaning backwards, and at the same time to raise his lever forearm across his face. Thus he is eventually lying face down with the broom parallel to his body but now on the opposite side. This gives him a wound up situation.

To unwind, the student pulls his lever hand across his face and down towards his thigh, his fulcrum hand staying in its original position throughout the whole process. This movement has brought the student to the position where he is lying on his back, and all that remains to complete the dry land roll is for him to sit up. After a little practice, it should not require a great deal of imagination to transfer the movements to a paddle and to get the feel of the canoe upside down, especially if the student has already learnt the basic swimming pool confidence building techniques.

If while attempting a Pawlata Roll, the paddler fails and finds himself lying upside down along the stern deck with his paddle alongside, he only has to use the Steyr method to roll upright. As with the Pawlata, the Steyr has been modified to what may be called a Steyr Across Roll, but this is only possible with a good hip action.

THE SCREW ROLL

The Screw Roll is similar to the Pawlata Across Roll except that the paddle is held in the normal paddling position, neither blade being extended (plate 8). In the learning stages, the rearward end of the paddle often becomes entangled with the canoe. This can be prevented by taking the whole paddle over the gunwale and pushing it downwards (as seen by the paddler when sitting in the upright position) with the fulcrum, or rearward, hand, while the lever, or forward, hand sweeps outwards taking the paddle in an arc across the surface of the water, with the leading edge angled upwards to give support. The movement can be assisted by taking the shoulders around so that the chest is facing towards the paddle whilst capsizing. The hip rotation is even more important than in the rolls where the paddle is extended as there is less leverage and support from the blade.

7. A teaching hand-grip which forces the canoeist to use his hips correctly

8. A Screw roll

The Screw Steyr Roll, or Reverse Screw Roll, is similar to the Screw except that the paddle stroke is started from the stern end in a backward leaning position. Most of the modern exponents tend with all the screw rolls to make them a Screw Across action which relies to a great extent on correct body movement.

THE STORM ROLL

The Storm Roll is not unlike the Pawlata Across Roll except that the paddle is taken down deep and perpendicular to the surface of the water. It was developed for use in white water which is fluffed up and gives little or no buoyancy. The lead up to this roll is a sculling movement with a perpendicular paddle, leaning more and more until the complete capsize position is reached and the recovery is achieved whilst the paddle remains upright. This is an advanced roll and requires good technique.

9. When the student can Eskimo roll successfully, he should try this paddle retrieving exercise. Throw away the paddle, swim to it in the canoe, put it in place and roll up

HAND ROLLING

Hand rolling was first achieved in this country in about 1961, and has since become a highly developed branch of rolling. It is a particular aim of most swimming pool rollers, and can even be done with one hand inside the spray cover so that only one hand is used for the actual roll (plates 10, 11, and 12). Success is dependent upon the principles of body control outlined earlier in this chapter.

In 1971 at the National Surf Championships held at Bude, Cornwall, some competitors were actually throwing away their paddles, controlling their canoes with their hands, and deliberately capsizing to show their skill and ability at hand rolling.

There is little doubt that this requires supreme nerve as well as skill, but it has some dangerous points as well. The paddle is the most efficient means of propelling and manœuvring the canoe and to get rid of it voluntarily is perhaps foolhardy. On the other hand, if a spare paddle is carried on deck and the paddle being used is lost for some reason (not that it should be), hand rolling could well be a life saver.

10. The beginning of a two-handed roll with the canoe on the point of balance

11. Another two-handed roll. The canoeist is wasting energy by bringing up his body too fast

12. A one-handed roll. Note the low head position essential to success

ROLLING FOR SURVIVAL

Rolling has now reached a high degree of development and there only remains one variation to be achieved and that is the 'No Hands Roll' which must surely be classed as a 'Circus stunt'—but let us not forget the original purpose of rolling as a survival technique. Rolling, to be successful, must be practised as often as possible, and particularly at the end of a long sea journey when the paddler is tired and weary. For it is when the body is tired and weary that a capsize is likely to happen, and to practise in conditions where if the roll is not successful it will only be embarrassing may well result in a better roll when conditions are less favourable. In the event of a real emergency roll, if it is not successful there is never a complaint.

3

Surf Canoeing

ALEX and CLARE ALLAN

SURF, of one sort or another, can be found almost anywhere provided two basic ingredients are present, the first being waves and the second water which is shallow in relation to the height of the waves. For enjoyment by the canoeist, however, it is necessary to add a few refinements to this basic formula, a gently shelving sandy beach, waves of the right size and a gentle off-shore breeze being considered the ideal. With these conditions a wave, formed perhaps many miles out to sea, feels the 'drag' of the bottom as it approaches the shore, slows down, steepens and eventually breaks when the depth of the water is roughly twice the height of the wave.

Given these ideal conditions, there are three distinct areas in which the surf canoeist can enjoy his sport. The steep but unbroken or 'green' waves offer what is probably the greatest attraction. The canoeist heads towards the shore, gives a few quick strokes with the paddle as the wave begins to lift his stern, and he is off on an exhilarating free ride, the only effort required being an occasional steering stroke with the paddle and a final lean into a telemark to turn off the wave as it begins to break and before heading out to sea once again.

For the more experienced, or the more adventurous paddler (and one with a strongly built canoe), the breaking wave itself provides opportunities for thrilling and spectacular acrobatic feats calling for quick reactions, split second timing and often a good head for heights!

Lastly, there is the area of broken water, between the 'break line' and the shore, where the wave, having spent its energy, quickly diminishes in size and loses its identity as it mingles turbulently with the returning debris of the previous wave. Known to surfers as the 'soup', there is little here to interest the expert, but for the beginner it is the ideal place to adjust to the new environment. Here he can learn to ride small waves, to use his paddle as a brace when caught broadside to them, and to sort himself out after the inevitable capsize.

The popular surfing beaches in Cornwall, North Devon, the South Western parts of Wales and the West Coast of Ireland owe their reputation to the fact that they face the broad expanses of an ocean and the waves reaching them may have travelled hundreds, even thousands, of miles, from disturbances way out in the Atlantic. At any one time there could be three or four different areas scattered throughout the ocean where high winds are building up the waves and a regular supply of surf is almost guaranteed to those beaches which are lucky enough to face in the right direction.

Beaches facing lesser expanses of water such as the English Channel, the Irish Sea or the North Sea have less chance of regular surf, as the area in which suitable waves can be generated is so much smaller and any swell built up quickly dies down once the wind which creates it abates.

The regularly spaced, 'glassy' waves of which the surfer's dreams are made, however, are not the only type in which the sport can be enjoyed, and a study of the various factors involved can help in understanding the sort of conditions which are likely to be found on a particular beach, on a particular day and even at a particular time.

LOCAL WIND

Often the strength and direction of the wind on the beach are the most important factors in influencing the surf. Provided waves are approaching the beach, a gentle offshore wind will usually improve the surf, making the wave fronts steeper, and consequently easier to ride, but at the same time delaying the breaking of the waves and making for longer runs. Strong offshore winds may make it impossible for the canoeist to paddle fast enough to catch the waves, but should he manage to accelerate down the face, the apparent strength of the wind will immediately increase, he will be almost blinded by the spray thrown up by his bow and he will have to be prepared for a considerable pounding if he sticks with the wave as it breaks. Smaller waves, however, may be held up by a strong offshore wind to such an extent that they never reach the beach.

Onshore winds make for irregular and unpredictable waves with uneven fronts. The canoeist's reactions must be quick, as the changing shape of the waves calls for frequent changes of speed and direction if he is to ride them for any distance. With stronger onshore winds the result is simply a rough sea, rather than surf in the recognised sense, with waves breaking, re-forming and breaking again time after time.

ORIGIN OF WAVES

Waves which have been built up by strong winds far out in the ocean travel great distances until they are far removed from the forces which brought them into being. They are sometimes known as 'old' waves and those which reach our shores provide the bulk of the surf on the Atlantic facing beaches. It can happen that old waves with widely differing points of origin arrive on the same beach at about the same time and interfere with each other. If the crests of two waves happen to coincide the result is seen as an extra large wave, but if the crest of one coincides with the trough of another the effect is for one to cancel out the other. This interference pattern is constantly changing, depending on the size and frequency of the waves. Winds blowing much nearer the shore create 'new' waves which are then super-imposed on the old waves, complicating matters still further. This interference between waves of varied origin explains why a 'set' of larger waves will suddenly arrive at the beach following a period of several minutes of comparative calm.

STEEPNESS OF THE BEACH

With a gradually shelving beach the point at which the effect of the bottom is first felt, and at which the wave begins to steepen, will be a considerable distance from the water's edge. There will also be quite a distance between the point at which the wave becomes steep enough to ride and the point at which it breaks. A steeply shelving beach, on the other hand, will only give the canoeist very short runs and the break line will be close to the water's edge. Even with a big wave the break may be only a matter of yards from the dry sand and as the wave crashes down its predecessor will be rushing back down the sand to form a strong undertow. A wave such as this is known as a 'dumper' and can provide a most unpleasant experience for a canoeist careless enough to be caught in it.

SHAPE OF BEACH AND COASTLINE

A completely straight beach will tend to have fairly uniform surf conditions throughout its length. Conversely, an irregularly shaped beach is unlikely to have a regular surf pattern. A beach which curves through 90 degrees, for instance, could be subject to a diagonally offshore wind at one end and a diagonally on-shore wind at the other. Headlands or off-lying islands or rocks can provide obstructions, preventing waves from reaching part of a beach. High cliffs immediately behind a beach can some-times provide protection from offshore winds, allowing good surfing on a day when the same wind makes surfing very hard work on adjacent beaches backed by flat land.

The shape of any coastline where surfing is a possibility, however, is very much affected by the state of the tide, which determines the position of the water's edge at any given time, and so these two factors cannot be considered in isolation.

HEIGHT OF THE TIDE

On most surf beaches the tidal range, i.e. the amount by which the water rises or falls during the course of one tide, is at least 12 feet, but on beaches in Jersey or the upper reaches of the Bristol Channel the range on a Spring tide can be as much as 35 or 40 feet. As the effect on waves of underlying banks, reefs, rocks and so on, depends on the depth of water over them, the state of the tide is thus seen to be of great importance.

Most beaches shelve fairly steeply near the high water mark and where this is the case dumping will occur when the tide is high. On other beaches sandbanks may be revealed at low water, producing dumpers when the tide is low, creating a false break line when they are covered by a few feet of water, or causing waves to steepen prematurely when the water is deeper, thus providing unusually long runs.

Rocks which are covered at most states of the tide may appear as an unwelcome hazard within the break line as the tide falls.

If at high tide the waves on a surf beach reach the base of a cliff, or a protective sea wall, they will rebound, following the normal laws of reflection. As the reflected waves meet the in-coming waves and the crests coincide, 'haystacks' are formed. These steepsided pinnacles of water can provide much amuse-ment for experienced surfers playing in the backlash from a wall. A normal forward run in this type of water is apt to end abruptly as the canoe is hit by a reflected wave, but it is possible to enjoy the unusual experience of running seawards on a reflected wave for some distance before being stopped short by an incoming wave.

There are beaches which, while completely open to the sea and offering good surf when the tide is fairly high, become practically landlocked and devoid of surf as the tide drops and reefs at the sides and outlying rocks become exposed.

RIP CURRENTS

Rip currents are found on many of the surfing beaches of the British Isles and provide escape channels to relieve the pressure of water thrown up on the beach by the waves. They can run at up to 3 or 4 knots and are usually to be seen at the sides of beaches, near rocks, or at places where large streams flow into the sea. This is not always the case and a wide beach may exhibit several rips in different places at the same time.

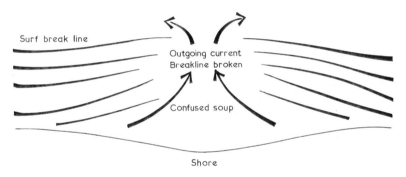

Fig. 8   Plan view of Rip Current

Rips are usually fairly easily recognised, particularly if viewed from a high vantage point and a calm space in the line of breaking waves is more than likely to be caused by an outgoing current (Fig. 8). Following a storm, or a particularly high tide, the position of the rips may change from one day to the next.

These currents present no particular hazard to a competent sea canoeist and may even be used to his advantage as an easy way out through the surf, as the outgoing flow of water often subdues the incoming waves. As the current reaches deeper water its strength is quickly dissipated. The best course of action for a canoeist who has baled out and is caught in a rip is to allow it to carry him and his canoe out beyond the break line and then to summon his colleagues to carry out a deep water rescue. If this course is impracticable, he should swim at right angles to the rip until he is out of it and make use of the normal incoming surf to help him back to the shore.

On beaches which are manned by a Lifeguard or by members of a Life Saving Club it is advisable to enquire about local hazards and to let the person in charge know your capabilities. A patrolled beach will probably have a bathing area marked by red and yellow flags and all canoeing should take place outside this section. Black and white chequered flags indicate an area reserved for malibu boards and surf canoes.

EQUIPMENT

Surf is powerful and unpredictable. It can snap a canoe in half; break a weak paddle; drag off an insecure crash hat. Faulty, unsuitable or badly fitting equipment could lead to a fatal accident.

Lifejackets
A Canoeist's Lifejacket conforming to the specifications of the British Standards Institute is the only type suitable for surf canoeing. The latest designs are fairly flat on the chest, do not impede movement, and yet in an emergency will keep the head above water even if the wearer is unconscious. An added advantage of the B.S.I. lifejacket is the protection given against possible blows by the buoyancy at the back of the neck. IT IS NOT CLEVER TO BE WITHOUT A LIFEJACKET, ONLY STUPID.

The buoyancy aids in other branches of canoeing are, as the name indicates, only an aid to buoyancy and if the wearer of one of these was to become unconscious through a blow on the head or neck, by being buried for a lengthy period under a large breaker, or through the effects of exhaustion or exposure, he could finish up floating face downwards.

Crash Hats
A crash hat is essential. Rocks below the surface are not the only hazard. A surf canoeist can be struck by his own canoe if he has to bale out. Other canoes or malibu boards in the area are potentially lethal weapons, which may get out of control at any moment.

Paddles
The beginner in surf will find flat blades easier to handle and control. Although the blades sometimes break in heavy surf they

are cheap and easily replaced. As the canoeist becomes more experienced he will probably find that oval loomed white water or slalom paddles, with curved blades, are preferable both for strength and for efficiency.

Spray Covers

A spray cover which fits tightly round both the canoe and the canoeist is necessary to prevent it from collapsing under the weight of a breaking wave. There must, however, be room in the 'sleeve' to allow the canoeist to twist his body and to lean forwards, backwards or sideways without pulling the spray cover off the cockpit rim. The most satisfactory spray cover for surf is made of nylon lined neoprene, as used for wetsuits. This material stretches and gives slightly in all directions. All spray covers should be fitted with release straps.

Canoes

With the exception of the 'surf board type canoe', which will be dealt with separately later in this chapter, no canoe has yet been produced specifically for surfing. The usual choice of surf canoeists in the British Isles at the time of writing is a G.R.P. slalom canoe. Other types of canoe, particularly white water and 'general purpose' boats can, provided they are strongly built and fitted with adequate buoyancy, be used as an introduction to surf canoeing, but once the basic techniques have been mastered in waves of moderate size, the need will be felt for a more manœuvrable craft in which the full potentialities of the sport can be realised.

Although no one design of slalom canoe is in particular favour, many of the most experienced surf canoeists in the country would probably agree with the following list of qualities required of a satisfactory surfing canoe:—

1. The canoe must react quickly to steering strokes with the paddle and must therefore have a well rockered keel. While some canoeists prefer a deep central section to their boat, however, others may be happier with a flatter sectioned boat. In choosing a canoe specially for surfing it is always advisable to try out as many different types as possible before making a final choice.

2. The canoe must be specially reinforced during manufacture in order to withstand the enormous pressure and pounding of the waves. Extra reinforcing added to a boat after it has been in use usually breaks away under the crushing effects of the

breakers. A finished weight of between 30 and 35 lbs. is recommended, although this could be reduced slightly if advantage is taken of modern materials such as carbon fibre or Diolen. A medium weight deck is adequate provided diagonal 'herring bone' reinforcing ribs are glassed in (Fig. 9), but the hull should have one more complete layer of glass fibre mat than is used for a boat intended for slalom competition.

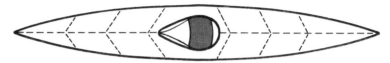

Fig. 9   Longitudinal and diagonal reinforcing of deck

A central strengthening rib running along the hull from end to end is necessary and longitudinal strengthening of the deck is also advised. The most important aid to the strength of the canoe is the use of 4-inch thick blocks of polyurethane or polystyrene foam placed vertically between the hull and the deck (Fig. 10). This should extend from the bow to the end of the footrest runners and from immediately aft of the cockpit to the stern. These blocks must be glassed in position to prevent being dislodged as the canoe flexes in heavy water. If one can confidently stand on the deck of one's canoe without fear of damage, then there is some hope of it being able to withstand the rigours of the surf.

Fig. 10   For buoyancy and strength—4 inch wide full length foam blocks

3. The foam blocks have a dual purpose in providing buoyancy as well as strength, but the buoyancy they provide is not sufficient in itself, and as much additional buoyancy as possible should be packed in the canoe and firmly secured. Inflatable bags and large polythene drums are most commonly used for this purpose.

4. The space forward of the footrest must be packed in such a way that it is impossible for the feet to pass over, under or beyond the footrest in the event of the footrest, or its supports, breaking. In a forward loop the canoeist stands with all his weight on the footrest and damage is a strong possibility.

5. Toggles should be fitted to both bow and stern. They provide handholds to enable a capsized canoeist to maintain control over his canoe while they are both being washed ashore through the surf, or as he awaits rescue by his fellow canoeists if he is beyond the break line. The loops sometimes fitted to slalom canoes can be dangerous in these circumstances as the fingers can be trapped if the canoe is rolled over by a wave.

6. Deck lines and 'paddle parks' are essential for sea and surf work, especially for group leaders or instructors. Deck lines, which provide convenient handholds on an otherwise slippery surface, greatly facilitate speedy rescue work in the event of a capsize. They must, however, be secured tightly and kept clear of the cockpit, a convenient method being shown in Figure 11.

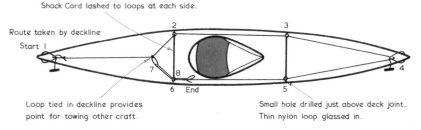

Shock Cord lashed to loops at each side.

Route taken by deckline

Start

Loop tied in deckline provides point for towing other craft.

Small hole drilled just above deck joint. Thin nylon loop glassed in.

Fig. 11   Decklines and paddle parks

Clothing

Although there may be rare days during the summer when it is possible to enjoy the surf protected only by a windproof anorak over normal canoeing clothing, for the fullest enjoyment of the sport a wetsuit is the only answer. A short sleeved suit may prove adequate for summer surfing, but during the winter months, when the surf is often at its best, a full wetsuit is essential not only for comfort but also for safety.

FIRST STEPS IN THE SURF

Before attempting to canoe in the surf the beginner should be able to perform the basic canoeing skills, particularly slap recovery stroke, sculling for support, draw stroke and methods of deep water rescue. Choose waves which are less than 3 feet in height, or if the surf is bigger than this stay well within the break line. Select an area of the beach which is free from rocks, rip currents, bathers, board riders and other canoeists and avoid strong off-shore winds and dumpers.

It is best to work in pairs, with one person on the beach and the other surfing. The beach man must watch his partner all the time and be ready to enter the water and give assistance as necessary. It is also advisable to have an experienced canoeist on the water to carry out a deep water rescue if the beginner capsizes beyond the break line or is swept out to sea by currents or wind.

If you have to bale out, hold on to the toggle at the seaward end of your canoe and push the canoe towards the shore, letting the waves help you. When standing in the water always keep to seaward of your canoe. Serious injuries have been caused by waves picking up canoes and hurling them against the owners' legs. Warn bystanders to keep clear, particularly small children who invariably crowd round and want to help.

Entering the Surf
Place your canoe facing the waves in a few inches of water and while it is still resting on the sand get in and secure your spray cover. Next, place your hands on the sand on both sides of the canoe and lift and ease the canoe forward until the water is deep enough to use the paddle. Head straight out to sea and keep paddling even when waves hit you. Do not go out too far, keeping well within the break line, then when in a trough turn your canoe broadside to the incoming waves ready to practise the paddle brace.

The Paddle Brace
As a wave reaches you, place the paddle flat on the surface over the oncoming wave and lean towards it. Depending on the size and strength of the wave, it will either pass under you or you will find yourself being carried sideways towards the shore. Practise this on both sides, in increasingly larger waves until you can take waves breaking at shoulder height. Try changing from a low brace (Fig. 12), with your paddle held at waist level, to a high brace (Fig. 13), where you lean more and hold the paddle at shoulder level. As your confidence develops try digging deep with your paddle and pulling yourself off a wave by using a strong draw stroke.

Running Forwards
Paddle out a short way, turn in a trough and point the canoe towards the beach. Choose a small wave and when it is a few

yards behind you start paddling forwards, accelerating and leaning forwards as it gets closer. When you are moving on the wave lean backwards to prevent the bow from digging in and use stern rudder strokes to steer the canoe straight towards the shore (Fig. 14). Only experience can tell you exactly when to start paddling and how much forward or backward leaning is necessary, as so much depends on the speed and steepness of the type of canoe you are using.

Fig. 12   Low Brace

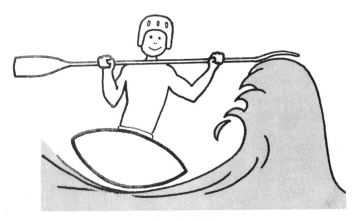

Fig. 13   High Brace

If insufficient force is applied to the stern rudder strokes, the canoe will swing rapidly sideways, so be prepared to lean towards the wave and adopt the paddle brace position. When running on a green wave, change from a stern rudder to a Telemark in order to turn off the wave just before it breaks.

Fig. 14   Stern Rudder Stroke

Running Backwards

This is the reverse of the previous technique. You will have to use bow rudder strokes, leaning well forward and placing the paddle blade close to the bow of your canoe. You will find that the canoe swings sideways much more violently than when running forwards and your reactions will have to be very quick if you are to steer a straight course.

The Eskimo Roll in Surf

Before progressing to more advanced surfing techniques it is essential to be able to roll. The secret of rolling in surf is to make use of the waves, in which case rolling can be easier than when in flat water, rather than fighting against the waves which makes a successful roll almost impossible. For your first attempt position your canoe broadside to the waves in 3 or 4 feet of of water. It at all apprehensive ask your partner to stand nearby. As a wave approaches prepare yourself for whichever roll you find easiest and capsize towards the beach. When the wave hits you roll up with your paddle on the seaward side. Practise this on both sides and when confident try a few rolls in the trough between the waves. When you are happy about being upside down in the surf, run forwards on a wave and as it breaks swing sideways and roll down the front. The wave will probably roll you up again before you know what has happened so be ready to paddle brace when you reach the surface.

Even while practising these basic surfing techniques there is a possibility of dangerous situations arising, but these can be avoided by following these simple rules:

1. Wear a crash hat and a lifejacket.
2. Do not canoe alone.
3. Before starting a run make sure the water ahead is free of other canoes, boards or bathers.
4. When paddling out through the surf keep clear of those surfing in.
5. If a collision seems likely, capsize immediately. The drag of your body will slow you down.
6. Only attempt deep water rescues outside the break line.
7. Take out Third Party Insurance.

ADVANCED TECHNIQUES

Paddling Out through Big Surf
In order to reach the green waves skill, strength and careful timing are necessary. When paddling through medium sized broken waves lean well back and keep paddling hard so that the canoe rides over, rather than through, the waves. If you find that some of the waves cannot be negotiated in this way you will have to hold back and make a dash for the break line in a lull between sets. If you think a wave is going to break just as you meet it, stop paddling and wait until it has broken before proceeding out to sea again. It is always tempting to race out in the hope of passing over a wave just before it breaks, but if mis-timed this can result in a rapid and undignified return towards the shore. If faced with a large wave about to break just in front of you, capsize immediately and the drag of your body may prevent you from being carried shorewards and you can then roll up. Make sure you take a good lung-full of air before attempting this manœuvre, however, because if it doesn't come off you will certainly need it.

Riding Green Waves
1. ZIG-ZAGGING. Start by running forward then swing from one side to the other, trying to get in as many changes of direction as possible before turning off the wave. It will be necessary to lean on your paddle, and of course downhill, as you apply your stern rudder strokes.
2. SHOULDERING. A wave does not always break along its whole length at one precise moment. Some waves will start to

break at one point and this point will then move along the face of the wave from one end to the other. The part of the wave which is just about to break is known as the shoulder and one of the most enjoyable ways of riding a wave is to run diagonally just ahead of it with the wave curling just behind (Fig. 15). You will have to use a strong stern rudder stroke on the downhill side to hold the canoe just below the crest of the wave.

Fig. 15   Shouldering away from the breaking part of the wave

3. ROLLER COASTING. This is possibly the fastest way of travelling in a canoe and with really good surf conditions can result in an exhilarating ride for several hundred yards along the face of a wave. Get up speed on a diagonal run and then let the canoe come as close as possible to the crest of the wave before leaning downhill and steering diagonally down again. Progress along the wave is made by repeating this sequence as frequently as the conditions allow.

Once you and your fellow canoeists have mastered the arts of zig-zagging, shouldering and roller-coasting, you can practise surfing in formation, or if you are looking for still more skills to tackle try carrying out all these manoeuvres in reverse.

Gymnastics on Breaking Waves
Before attempting the following techniques the canoeist must ensure that his canoe can be held firmly at knees and hips and that his footrest is correctly adjusted.

To achieve success the canoe must be running absolutely straight at the moment the wave breaks. The action of standing a canoe on end is generally referred to as a 'loop', but this could embrace any one of the following:

NOSE DIVE. Once you have plucked up the courage to hold the canoe straight as the wave breaks this is the most likely result, unless the waves are more than about three feet in height. The bow digs in, the stern lifts and the larger the wave, the nearer one approaches the vertical before the canoe drops back as the wave passes under it. (Fig. 16)

Fig. 16 Nose Dive

FORWARD LOOP. This is always exciting. Your first loop is nearly always accidental, but is sure to raise a big cheer from your friends! The forward loop is simply a forward somersault and is achieved by leaning well forward as the bow digs in, at the same time bringing the paddle alongside the canoe in preparation for a screw roll. When the wave passes the canoe is left upside down and after rolling up should be facing straight out to sea (Fig. 17).

DRY LOOP OR 'FLICK'. This starts off in the same way as a forward loop but when in a vertical position lean backwards and rotate the canoe through 180 degrees so that when the somersault has been completed the canoe is the right way up and facing out to

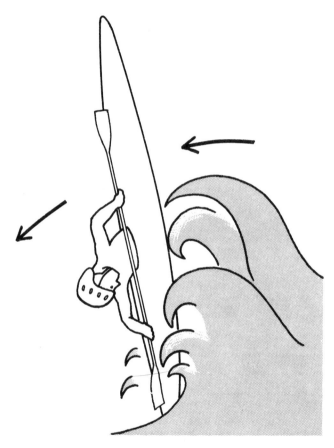

Fig. 17   Forward Loop

sea (Fig. 18). The rotation is mainly achieved by a twist of the body but once the movement has begun, further control may be gained by reaching down and putting the end of the paddle in the water.

When you first attempt a flick you will probably only manage a 90 degree twist, the result being simply a nose dive followed by a sideways fall, but with luck you will remain dry.

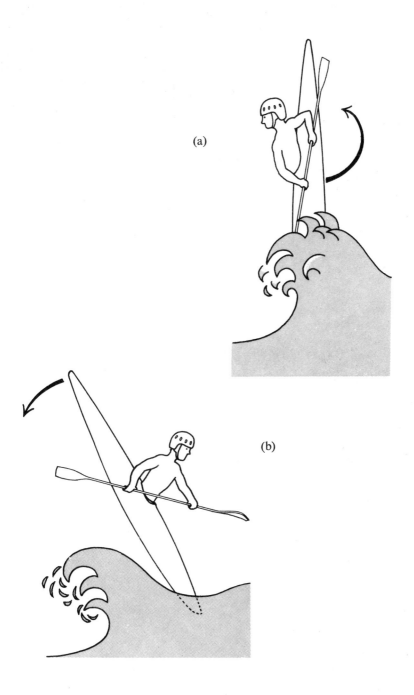

Fig. 18 Dry Loop or 'Flick' (a) Vertical Nose dive followed by 180° twist
(b) Drop down facing seawards

PIROUETTE OR 'SPIN'. One of the most advanced skills is the ability to rotate a canoe through 360 degrees or more while it is in a vertical position. Although at the time of writing only one canoeist is known to have achieved as many as two and a half rotations and still come down the right way up, with the present rate of progress in this branch of canoeing, feats such as this could well become commonplace in years to come. An interest ing and possibly a more skilful variation is to spin the canoe through 360 degrees while it is in a shallow nose dive.

'POP-OUT' OR SKY ROCKET. These terms are used when the canoe leaves the water completely as it is in vertical position, whether it be during a nose dive, a flick or a pirouette. The secret is to poise the canoe momentarily on the crest of the wave and then to dive straight off the top as it breaks. A canoe with buoyant bow sections is more likely to become airborne in this way.

'POLEVAULTING'. If the bow of the canoe hits the sand while performing any of the techniques described above, the result is described as a Pole Vault. Often when the waves are too small for normal looping it is still possible by polevaulting to reach the vertical position.

REVERSE LOOPS. All the above should theoretically be possible in reverse. Reverse Loops and 'Stern Dives' are frequently performed, while the rarer Reverse Flick, followed immediately by a forward run on the same wave, is one of the most satisfying experiences in surf canoeing. Reverse Polevaulting is not recommended, because of possible danger to the spine.

Riding Broken Waves

Maintaining control over the direction of the canoe while being carried in on a broken wave is of importance for safety reasons and should be practised as much as possible. When surfing broadside on a wave, once the canoe is balanced satisfactorily, the paddle can be used not only for bracing but also to propel the boat forwards or backwards along the face of the wave. As the strength of the wave subsides it is usual to lean heavily on the paddle and to turn off the wave, but a competent canoeist should also be able to turn towards the shore and continue running on the broken wave. Running straight is not possible on really powerful broken waves, but these can provide opportunities for loops, flicks etc., which are normally performed as the wave first breaks.

Although many of the skills described under the heading of

Advanced Techniques have been dealt with in isolation, much of the fun of surf canoeing stems from the ability of the canoeist to combine a variety of manœuvres on the same wave.

'SURF BOARD TYPE' CANOES

The surf board type canoe (for which no satisfactory name has yet been invented) is designed specifically for surfing and combines the characteristics of both a slalom and a malibu board. It originated on the coast of California, where it evolved from the surf ski, which is a long skeg-less board propelled with a paddle. It is rapidly gaining popularity on our surf beaches and has also proved to be highly successful in riding the Severn Bore. It has a flat bottomed hull which curves up towards the bow, similar to a board, but has a deck and cockpit as in a kayak. Present designs have a length of about 7 feet and a beam of about 22 inches (Fig. 19).

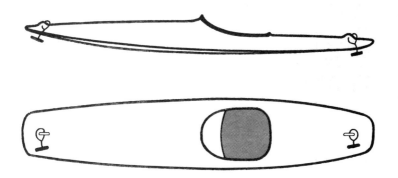

Fig. 19   A 'surf board type' canoe

The same paddling techniques are used as with a conventional canoe. Most of the normal surf canoeing manœuvres can be carried out, but this type of canoe will turn faster, run at a finer angle to the wave (and thus faster) and ride steeper waves without the bow digging in. Turns of 360 degrees on the face of the wave are possible and it will also run before large breaking waves. Although designed not to loop, forward loops are not too difficult to achieve and reverse loops are relatively easy.

The surf board type canoe is slow to paddle on flat water but its turned up nose gives it certain advantages when paddling out over broken waves.

Because of the differences in performance, surf board type canoes and slalom canoes are classed separately in Surf Canoeing competitions.

LIFESAVING METHODS FOR CANOEISTS

Any party of surf canoeists should be completely independent and able to extricate themselves from any potentially dangerous situation which may arise. Furthermore, because of their ability to paddle quickly through broken water they could easily be the first helpers to reach a bather in difficulty and they should know what to do when they arrive.

The few simple rescue methods described here have been developed by members of the Corps of Canoe Lifeguards and can be carried out by any competent canoeist. Every opportunity should be taken to practise them. This is not only good fun but at some future date might result in the life of a canoeist or a bather being saved.

Dealing with a Conscious Patient

STERN CARRY (Fig. 20).

Fig. 20   Stern Carry

The best method when the patient is fully co-operative. Particularly useful for helping fellow canoeists. Try this in big surf, both as rescuer and as patient.

BOW CARRY (Fig. 21).
Use for a tired or frightened patient. You can see and talk to him and little effort is required on his part.

Warning! Always approach a panicky swimmer with great caution—he may well try to clamber on top of you. If in doubt, avoid contact until he has calmed down.

If coming ashore through surf, approach stern first, paddle into breaking waves to prevent running.

Fig. 21 Bow Carry

Unconscious Patient

RESUSCITATION IN THE WATER (Fig. 22).

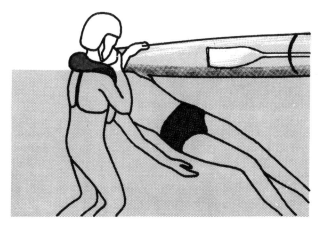

Fig. 22 Resuscitation in the water using the bow of the canoe for support

Park paddle, jump out taking care not to capsize, swim with canoe to patient. With one hand on end of canoe, force patient's head backwards over your arm, commence mouth-to-nose resuscitation.

RESUSCITATION ON A RAFT

Raft alongside patient. Nearest canoeist turn patient to face raft. Second canoeist reach across to grasp patient's wrists. (Fig. 23a). Pull patient across raft, turn face upwards. Begin resuscitation (Fig. 23b).

Canoeist Trapped in Canoe

A canoeist may be found upside down, trapped in his canoe. Lean across upturned canoe, grab victim's arm and roll him

(a)
(b)

Fig. 23   Two man raft and resuscitation

upright. If patient is unconscious, force his trunk and head as far back as possible, lean across and begin resuscitation while holding two canoes close together. (Fig. 24).

Fig. 24   Resuscitating the trapped canoeist

Always remember that the first priority in dealing with a tired or an unconscious patient is to give support, and resuscitation if necessary. If there is surf of even moderate size you may not be able to bring him ashore, but must summon further assistance. Methods of signalling and further information on canoe rescue work can be found in the manual of the Corps of Canoe Lifeguards.

COMPETITIVE SURF CANOEING

Every year since 1965 National Surf Canoeing Championships have been held at Bude in North Cornwall. Organised by members of the B.C.U., the competitions are held during the Surf Canoeing Week, a popular event which attracts ever increasing numbers of canoeists and their families to this friendly resort. In more recent years, local Surf Canoeing competitions have also been held in other parts of the country.

The following are the main events in the National Championships, but on occasions substitute events have been used due to abnormal weather conditions which produced either flat calm conditions or impossibly rough seas.

1. Canoe Handling—Junior, Ladies and Open
2. Surf Board Type Canoe Handling—Open
3. Surf Race (Slalom Canoes)—Junior, Ladies and Open
4. Team Relay Race.

Points gained in the above count towards a trophy competed for by teams from B.C.U. affiliated clubs.

The Canoe Handling competition is the premier event in the programme for any competition, whether National or Regional. Judging this event is no easy task. It is impossible to use judging techniques as used in, for example, skating or gymnastics. In these sports the conditions under which the competitors perform are static, so each competitor can be judged individually, performing set skills under identical conditions. In surf the conditions vary so much during the course of a day, or even from hour to hour, that instead of competing individually, a number of competitors are judged together in a heat. What they achieve in that heat is not related to the performance of another group in another heat. Usually the first two or three in each heat move forward to the next round. There should be seven judges, each responsible for one of the following sections:

(a) Style and Poise. Does the competitor look at home and at ease in the surf?

(b) Manœuvrability. Does the competitor have full control over his canoe? Has he a purpose in performing a certain manœuvre whether it be a turn or a roll?

(c) Sportsmanship. The competitor will lose points if he puts off, or obstructs, a fellow competitor in any way, or if he fails to offer help to anyone in difficulty.

(*d*) Safety. Does the competitor make a definite move to avoid a collision? Does he capsize to stop himself moving if a collision seems inevitable?

(*e*) Running on a Wave. The competitor is judged on his ability to ride any sort of wave.

(*f*) 'Aquanastics'. Loops, Flicks, Nose Dives, Pirouettes etc.

(*g*) Control and Surfmanship. The competitor's ability to 'read' the water. Can he anticipate what the surf is likely to do so that he is not accidentally caught out by the wave when he is trying to perform a particular manœuvre?

Each judge is watching and comparing all the competitors. Some aspects of judging overlap but all the judges work independently until the end of the heat, when they may consult together as to the final order of the competitors.

Competitors in the National Championships are bound by the following Safety Rules:

1. All competitors must be able to roll in surf.

2. Lifejackets and crash hats must be worn.

3. Canoes must be packed with extra buoyancy so that control can be retained even if the spray cover is off and the canoe is completely waterlogged.

4. Canoes must be equipped in such a way that it is impossible for the competitor's feet to pass beyond the footrest in the event of the footrest or its support breaking.

5. Canoes must be fitted with toggles at each end.

6. All competitors must be covered for Third Party Insurance.

During the National Championships members of the Corps of Canoe Lifeguards provide safety patrols, both on the shore and on the water.

4

Inland Touring

KATHLEEN TOOTILL

ONE day just before World War II a little knot of people stood on the shore at Durdle Door in Dorset. The object of their curiosity was a man and wife with a salt-stained, beamy, double canvas canoe. They were touring and they had just rounded Portland Bill. Their aim was to paddle right round Great Britain. More than 100 years ago John (Rob Roy) MacGregor stirred imagination with his long canoe voyages on European rivers. Today probably the majority of canoes are used locally, for day runs, for competition, or for messing about in odd leisure hours. But for those with the urge to rove, the possession of a canoe can mean adventurous travel limited only by the water available.

In these days of specialized canoes, with hulls adapted for straight racing, for slalom, for rivers rapid or slow, or for the sea, the intending tourist will have to decide on a compromise model. His primary need is for adequate space to carry baggage, but he does not want in achieving this to sacrifice all the speed and lightness of the racer, nor the manœuvrability of the slalom canoe, for his way may lie along the placid Thames or a turbulent mountain fed river, and in Britain especially with its superb coastline he will surely want to travel on the sea also. A rough guide to this compromise boat that is to be used on all waters not of extreme difficulty suggests a length of 14 feet or thereabouts, 24–26-inch beam and a slightly rockered bottom.

Britain, however, may be only part of the picture, for to find rivers long enough for a fortnight's holiday one must go abroad, at least to Europe, and this will suggest the advantages of a folding canoe for both convenience of stowage and cheapness of transport to the chosen river. The intending tourist who is also a specialist need not be debarred from using his specialized canoe, but his racer will deter him from rocky rapids and his well-rockered slalom boat may be slow and tiring on

13. The Ardèche River in Southern France is certainly the most popular
of all touring rivers for the canoeist. From Vallon to St Martin there is
three days of paddling through the massive Ardèche Gorge. For the
canoeist who wants a longer tour, a start can be made from Vogue higher
up the river, but from this start there are a number of weirs with difficult
portages along the route

the long flat stretches encountered on most big rivers; wind and
waves on slow rivers and canals, and, of course, on sea and
estuary, will play havoc with his steering unless he adds a rudder.
Double canoes, although proportionately fewer nowadays,
crewed by those who know how to work together, can be a joy
on wide river and sea and will considerably reduce physical
effort. Photographers know the advantage of paddling a double,

with one partner controlling the boat while the other presses the trigger; and, of course, with shared camping gear, and the ample stowage space canoe-camping in a double is quite luxurious. But there are excellent and spacious single touring canoes.

The modern tendency is for cockpits to be as small as is compatible with the operation of getting in and out. This means a smaller area of spray cover and a nearer approach to watertightness. But the touring canoeist may prefer a larger cockpit. He is not in a hurry and his object is enjoyment of travel. He wants his equipment to be accessible without having to grope for it, and the larger cockpit facilitates the management of camera, sketching materials, a bird book maybe and a monocular or field glasses, maps and guides, casual food and drink. It is pleasant also to let the sunshine on to one's legs. For the deeper stretches of exposed waters, and for the sea, the double canoe and the long single-seater should have a rudder so that when the wind or waves are on a quarter one can still put equal pressure on either end of the paddle instead of having to overwork one side.

To camp on a canoe tour is not essential: many continental rivers have chains of youth hostels or canoe stations at suitable distances, and in this country some people rely on the village inn. But camping brings freedom of movement and relief from anxiety should the day's programme be interrupted. It is not always possible to judge the distance to be covered in one day, for winds, high or low water, tides, and, of course, the occasional capsize or holed boat, can make a difference sometimes amounting to hours. Again, during the day one may want to linger in some spot or exploie awhile on foot, and the knowledge thatt house and home are stowed below decks makes one carefree. In any case the canoeist who camps experiences pleasure immeasurable: to pitch tent close to the water, boat at hand, to fall asleep to the sound of water, for even the quiet river has its subtle music, to wake next day entranced by those same sounds, mingled with the early calls of birds and water creatures; such things give the canoe-camper full enjoyment. Camping makes things give the down the remoter rivers inaccessible to road users and house dwellers.

The intending canoe-camper who has already cycle-camped or pedestrian-camped will have no difficulty in selecting his equipment. The canoe will take rather more bulk and weight than the pedestrian carries on his back, but those who travel light gain greatly when, for instance, portaging round a weir or unshootable fall, when arriving and departing from camp, especially if the bank is steep, and of course when paddling, for a heavily laden boat rides a little lower in the water. Only experience and experiment will provide each canoeist with his ideal camping equipment, but if he thinks in terms of house, bed, kitchen, food, light, clothing, hygiene and hobbies he will have no real difficulty—but the camper who canoes does have a few points to consider beyond those of the plain camper.

House. As the morning pack-up may be wet, a tent with nylon or Terylene flysheet is an advantage, for everything else stays dry and the small wet roll can be stowed separately or can be dried out in a few minutes if the rain stops. A sewn-in groundsheet is invaluable if the river rises unexpectedly in the night and camp has to be shifted, for the whole tent and all in it can be picked up and moved at one go.

Bed. If the sleeping-bag is not quite warm enough, as good as an extra blanket is a long scarf wound round your middle, and this has daytime use as well. Insignificant as regards bulk and weight is the 'space blanket', a large sheet of polythene silvered on both sides. This at hand in the small hours when the air is at its chilliest quickly restores warmth.

Kitchen. Except in really wild country or below river banks, fires are not often allowed nowadays. The half-pint pressure stove is probably the most convenient and economical cooker for the lightweighter. Undoubtedly more popular today is the smallest edition of 'bottled gas', but refills are expensive and the empties present a disposal problem. All food and matches must be in waterproof containers. Polythene bags are good, but these should be kept within tins or some other strong containers. Remember a rat or a cat may drop in for a midnight feast!

Food. Canned food is heavy and bulky; there are so many dehydrated foods available that provisioning is no problem. It is important to think ahead about drinking water and, for safety, carry some on the voyage.

Light. In summer a torch is adequate in Britain. Farther south, or in spring and autumn a supply of candles is useful.

Clothing. Continuous paddling encourages warmth but stopping to eat can be chilling, so several light layers, according to season, are better than one thicker garment, and a light waterproof anorak should be at hand. Some people prefer the freedom of a sou'wester to the anorak hood which may dull the hearing. Plastic sandals, or gym shoes with a few holes to let out the water, are good to wear when canoeing, but for a long stretch in the canoe they can be exchanged for thick woollen socks. Gum boots are bulky and dangerous for a canoeist. A towel, warm jersey and trousers must be carried in case of capsize. In the event of a second capsize there are always one's pyjamas, but there must be no third ducking!

A large very thin polythene bag kept in the pocket makes an excellent tent for that midday halt in a biting wind or for the victim of a capsize for whom it can be almost a life saver.

Hygiene. Unless it is known that all camp sites to be used have sanitary arrangements laid on, it is essential for a canoeing party to carry a latrine tent and entrenching tool and to dig only where other tents will not be pitched. For small parties camping only in wild or remote country the minimum necessity is that each person should carry a knife or small trowel and dig for himself. Neglect of this duty may endanger other people's health.

Hobbies. Photographers, sketchers, bird watchers, geologists and writers need not leave their tools at home. Everything that is carried in a canoe should be tied up in a waterproof bag.

Normal buoyancy equipment for a canoe is roughly that of a gallon polythene bottle secured inside each end. With the added weight of camping gear it is advisable to imprison a little air in each of the waterproof bags containing the gear, especially in such things as air pillows. All the gear bags, in addition to being effectively closed, must be tied or securely jammed into the canoe. There are various ways of packing. It is usual to put most of the weight into the ends of the boat, but it should be noted that excessive weight at the ends make the boat less manœuvrable, while much weight amidships, added to that of the paddler, may make the ends swivel too easily. Weight must be distributed so that the canoe rides horizontally. Some people add a long string to packages thrust into the ends, as otherwise they may have to upend the boat to get them out. A package tied to the floor just in front of the seat provides a good relaxing support for the knees. Common sense directs that anything that might be needed during the day, including a canoe repair outfit, should be readily accessible and that the first requisite at the end of the journey, the tent, should be easily at hand. The painter and its fastening must be beyond reproach, for when you make a lunch halt you may not want to lift the laden canoe from the water, and you may have to tie up in a current. If it should be decided to carry the canoe complete with load, it is well to have four carriers, two supporting the cockpit region so as not to strain the shape of the canoe.

Before launching it is important to remember that in Britain many of the rivers used freely by canoeists until about 1966 are now claimed for sole use by anglers. The Sports Council whose aim is to secure the maximum use of natural resources for recreation, is aware of the dilemma of the touring canoeist, but in 1972 there is still no sign of an arrangement by which the harmless traveller by canoe can regain his lost rivers. On rivers where there is an established right of navigation, such as the Wye below Hay and the Severn from Poole Quay there is no difficulty, while those controlled by British Waterways or the Thames Conservancy are available by licence.

Canoeists already experienced in local paddling, and equipped with canoe and camping gear, will take off on experimental tours without difficulty, and after even one weekend will have learnt more than any book could teach. But the inquirer who has not yet tried the game may like to go first on some organized holiday with all equipment provided. The advantage of starting this way is that you are helped to decide whether to commit yourself to the purchase of your own equipment (the answer is seldom in doubt!) and that you build up enough knowledge to enable you to buy or make the right kind of equipment adapted to your own individuality. Several travel organizations—e.g., The Holiday Fellowship, 142 Great North Way, Hendon, London, N.W.4; the Youth Hostels Association, Trevelyan House, St Albans, Herts—include canoe-camping tours in their programmes. Another one, P. G. L. Voyages Ltd., specializes in the organisation of canoe-camping holidays, at home and abroad. For more formal courses, the Central Council of Physical Recreation, 26–29 Park Crescent, London, W.1 should be approached. Every Easter weekend Britain's largest touring club, The Canoe Camping Club (11 Lower Grosvenor Place, London, S.W.1), holds a meet on some easy but interesting river, often the Wye, Severn, Trent, Thames or Great Ouse, when up to 120 canoe-campers may gather. They come and camp for the four days, tyros and old hands together, young and old, one vast friendly company, and anyone wishing to learn the game could hardly do better than turn up there, even just to be among the vast variety of canoes, tents and gadgets, and mingle with the experience of many waters in many lands. Scouts will already know of the famous Scout cruises run annually by Percy Blandford, who needs no introduction.

But enough of preparation. Let us get afloat and travel. Unless you have already done it with one of the above organizations the Wye is an excellent starter. Do not attempt the rocky upper part but launch at Glasbury. From there to Chepstow are about 100 miles of river without the need for a single portage, easy but with simple manageable rapids occasionally and with the interesting estuarial run on the last day from Tintern to Chepstow when tides must be studied and the run made on the ebb. A special canoeist's map of the Wye is published by P. W. Blandford. For England and Wales in general, get a copy of Stanford's *Canoeing Map of England and Wales,* and for Ireland, *Canoeist's Map of Ireland* (a *Canoeing* publication). Practically the whole of the British Isles is covered in the British Canoe Union's Guide to the Waterways of the British Isles. This, and in fact most of the canoeing maps also, British and foreign, can be bought from BCU Supplies, 26–29 Park Crescent, London, W.1. It must be remembered that the mention of a river in these publications is nowadays no proof that you will be allowed on it.

When planning your tour you will want to know, how far shall I manage in a day? This is a hard question to answer, for much depends on conditions—speed of water, wind, number of portages, number of hours available for canoeing; whether you like a lazy morning striking camp, enabling the dew to dry off your tent, or an early evening pitching. There is time to be allowed for off-the-river excursions, and there is always the chance of a puncture or a capsize, so a firm estimate is impossible. But *do* start at least one day at dawn! A rough though arbitrary guide to progress is that your pace on a fairly sluggish river may be about that of yourself as pedestrian. For fast rivers add to your speed the speed of the current.

The Severn can be canoed from Llanidloes, but if on a first voyage you want to avoid hazards, start at Welshpool. With the exception of portages at two or three weirs you will have an uninterrupted run of great interest for varied water conditions and scenery as far as Worcester, a distance of just over 100 miles. Below Worcester there is less interest until Gloucester, where the Severn becomes tidal, and these estuarial waters, which provide great variety of experience for the really able canoeist, need most careful study beforehand, particularly because of the exciting bore which at the fortnightly spring tides could be dangerous to the unpractised canoeist. For the non-tidal part of the Severn below Stourbridge a licence is now required from British Waterways.

If further exploration of the quieter rivers is sought, there is the Thames in its gentle and lovely valley—wild river only from Cricklade to Lechlade, thereafter a locked navigation down to Teddington. A licence from the Thames Conservancy is required for this stretch. The voyage can be continued down the tideway to Greenwich or farther if the paddler has some knowledge of tides, estuarial conditions and shipping lanes. The Warwickshire Avon, the Trent, and the Great Ouse are rivers all long enough for a cruise of several days.

For the quiet-water canoeist who likes good scenery, Ireland has much to offer. By canal and the river Shannon it is possible to go from east coast to west (Dublin to Limerick), or to do the length of the Shannon from Lough Allen. Dublin to Waterford is possible by canal and river, while the length of the Blackwater (Cork) makes an ideal cruise comparable in scenery and water to our Wye.

The newcomer to rapid rivers should remember that guidebook descriptions of rapids and other hazards are usually of what may be called average conditions and that, because they are mountain-fed rivers and have considerable gradient, water levels vary tremendously; whereas after a dry spell much wading may be necessary, particularly with a loaded boat, flood conditions, which are often sudden, may be difficult and even unmanageable for those used only to quiet water. However easy the water is when the day's run begins, precautions must never be relaxed—all gear must be firmly secured, spray cover in order and lifejacket worn. Then in the event of a capsize the day can continue to be one of happy adventure. There was once a miserable chap who lost everything on the first day of a fortnight's holiday! It is assumed that no one will venture on a rapid river without knowing what to do with a canoe caught on a rock or against the pier of a bridge and in danger of breaking or of wrapping itself round a tree trunk, though the trained canoeist should usually be able to avoid getting into such troubles. Baggage and ropes must be stowed so as not to entangle the legs, and the spray cover must be self-releasing from either boat or person, but not from both or it will be lost. While in Scotland it is certainly worthwhile to cruise down the Tay from Loch Tay. The voyage can be continued past Perth down the Firth of Tay to finish at perhaps Dundee or beyond. On the Tay are many quiet stretches, but the hazards at Grantully, Campsie Linn (in high water), and Stanley Weir demand great care. I have seen several canoes wrecked at Grantully and I personally find it comforting first to unload my camping gear on to the bank a little way above, afterwards retrieving it by walking back and re-stowing it in the calm water well below the bridge. Again, while in Scotland, if there is time, make that rewarding trip through the Walter Scott country down the Tweed, launching perhaps at Peebles. The Tweed has some exciting rapids and shootable caulds (weirs) and it is advisable to stop and prospect some of them, notably the ones at Makerston, before committing oneself with a loaded canoe.

Apart from these rivers of considerable volume it should be borne in mind that most of Britain's rapid rivers, except after a distinctly rainy period, may offer a number of rocky rapids too shallow for a laden touring canoe, and whereas wading and towing for occasional short distances may be a pleasant game, too much of it is wearying, and the extra inches below water-line of a laden boat may cause a deal of wading unnecessary with an empty canoe. An exception among rapid rivers is the Welsh Teifi which, being fed from marshy uplands, is rarely very low and provides a delightful and exciting run from Tregaron down to the sea.

Every year great numbers of canoe-campers plan to do their touring abroad. In addition to the natural desire to see more of the world there is the lure of bigger and more exciting rivers and the knowledge that there will be no question of trespass. Little wonder that we are abandoning home waters for the more friendly foreign river life.

So let us see what Europe has to offer. Those who prefer to start their continental canoeing with a group can, as for the Wye at home, join one of the organizations mentioned above and tour with all equipment provided, largely on popular rivers such as the Rhône, Rhine, Mosel and Danube. The BCU has made arrangements to take parties by coach with a trailer equipped to carry the canoes, for tours of French and German and possibly other rivers. Members of these parties take their own equipment. Outside these organizations there is the choice of using public transport or taking one's own car to reach the river. If there is but one car in the party and no non-canoeing driver, the car will be abandoned at the start of the voyage and there is the matter of getting back to it. But river valleys are often bus and train routes, so the driver can usually find some way of getting back to his car. When a party has two or more cars a popular, though time-consuming, method is for at least two cars to be taken to the proposed end of the voyage and one of them to return to the start carrying both or all the drivers. Then when the voyage is ended there will be at least one waiting car, which will immediately convey back the other drivers so as to bring all cars to the end to be loaded. The advantage of using public transport is the avoidance of all this car shuttling, which few people really enjoy. Continental trains are accustomed to carrying rigid canoes, but buses can manage only folding ones. The Touring Club de France, 62 Avenue Parmentier, Paris 11e, has done a great deal for canoeing, producing specialized maps and guides. In that country there are rivers to suit every taste although, as almost everywhere else nowadays, hydro-electric barrages are becoming more numerous spoiling long stretches of water for the canoeist and necessitating often laborious portages. For this reason an essential part of one's equipment, unless it is known that there will be no long portages, is a small folding trolley carried in the canoe or strapped on the deck.

For a start in France, try the river with the most magnificent, even startling scenery, the Ardèche. It rises in the Cevennes country, scene of R. L. Stevenson's travels with Modestine, and winds eastwards through a stupendous gorge to join the Rhône near Pont St Esprit. The wonderful thing about this river is that, running in places between enormous vertical cliffs where one might expect unshootable torrents, it is actually easy enough for a beginner and its sparkling little rapids need cause no alarm in summer time except after a phenomenal storm; in this case even camping is dangerous, for the river rises at an incredible pace, and from a camp on a ledge in the gorge, a favourite place, there would be no escape except by water. On one memorable occasion, reading the portents, we put a canoe by each tent, then about midnight, when the flood came, each tent was moved intact with contents and bundled into a canoe. Luckily, on this occasion there was a

14. Lining down a shallow rapid on a very low River Tarn in Southern France. This river should be of grade III but by mid-summer most rapids are of only a poor grade II. A very fine river for the touring canoeist, giving some five days of interesting canoeing through the Gorge du Tarn, with the best water to be found during March to May

higher terrace to which it was possible to carry everything. Paddling through the main gorge takes two to three days. The lightest camp equipment is all that is needed and it is quite usual not to bother to pitch tent but to lie out on the flat sunbaked slabs of rock. A store of local grapes and peaches, a yard or two of French bread, will stave off the wolf, but it is as well to take a large water-carrier, for drinking water is obtainable at only two springs in the gorge. The river is literally thick with fish. At one point it is bridged by a natural arch, the Pont d'Arc, where the water has cut through a limestone cliff and the prehistoric ox bow now dry can be viewed from the cliff top. Naturally, a superb journey like this is popular, and dozens of canoes of many nationalities pass down the gorge every day. That adds to the interest, and by the time you have exchanged ideas with these many new friends you will have no need of further advice

15. Cruising on the River Hornad in Czechoslovakia

on continental rivers from books for you will get it first hand. If you do not capsize accidentally on the Ardèche, you will probably do it on purpose—for the delicious cooling swim. Lower down the Rhône, on the left bank, comes in the Durance. This is a river very different from the Ardèche. Rising in the Alpes Hautes near Briançon and the Italian border, its milky glacial waters rush down an Alpine valley, in places at a good gradient, giving quite formidable rapids. Rapid river experience is desirable before an attempt is made on this river, and capsize drill should be familiar, for immersion in these icy waters could be harmful, even lethal. About 35 km. down from l'Argentière, a good starting point, the river wells up into a huge reservoir entailing a 12 km. portage, but it is well worth starting again below down the still exciting current and continuing to the Rhône junction, though the last day's journey is on slow water. The Rhône itself used to provide an excellent longish cruise from near the Swiss border to the Mediterranean, but in recent years several barrages have been built, necessitating lengthy portages and making the water more sluggish. These French examples are only a few. There are other good rivers joining the Rhône, and farther west those of the Gironde basin, for example the Tarn, Dordogne, Lot and the pleasant but less exciting rivers that join the Loire, are worth consideration. Take a good map of France, plan your tour, then write to the T.C.F. for advice and details of your proposed rivers.

Germany, Austria, northern Italy, Yugoslavia, Poland, Spain, Sweden, to mention only a few, have a wealth of canoeable rivers, and all have organizations which will help the British canoeist. A list is given in Appendix II. These countries have their rivers graded according to an international code and this will help your selection. Several countries organize international canoe touring events at which you will be welcomed. For example, in Austria one can go to a base camp on the Chiem See, whence coach parties are taken daily under leaders to launching spots on rivers of various grading, so that one can progress daily to more advanced paddling.

Perhaps you are more adventurous than to want merely to join other canoeists or even to paddle the well-known rivers. Does the unknown attract you? I have been lucky on several occasions in finding companions who were keen to pioneer new routes for canoeists. In 1952 we were probably the first

west European canoeists to paddle the Yugoslavian Drinat
In 1957 we went to find the possibilities of Iceland and had
thrilling voyages down the Hvita, the Thegandi and the Blanda.

16. An early morning paddle on the River Arno, in Florence. In the
background the famous Ponte Vecchio

We found many rivers which will provide first-class experience
for future canoeists once they can overcome travel difficulties in
a land so lacking in roads that ponies and planes are the most
usual way of getting about. Bulgaria in 1963 was another venture
into a land where canoeing had been limited to a large reservoir
made by the Stalin dam on the river Iskar near Sofia. There we
had a wildly exciting run down the Rilske and the Struma and
a quieter but more beautiful run along the Kamchiya and into
the Black Sea. At that time wild camping was illegal but we
willingly endured three hours' arrest for the privilege! The long
river Maritza, not fully explored by us, suggests an admirable
canoe-camping journey.

Since the summer of 1968 British canoe-campers have had friendly links with their Finnish counterparts and have shared with them annually unforgettable wilderness voyages in the bright warm Lapland summer, travelling maybe up to 250 miles down one river, whole days of continuous, but mostly easy rapids, with occasional lakes in between.

Although most European countries now have their canoe organizations and there are not, therefore, many still unvisited by Britons, there remain, for those with the initiative to seek them out, many remote rivers, on which canoe has not yet floated. Europe is of course not the limit. Canoeists in Australia, New Zealand, Canada, the USA, Africa and South America have already blazed trails for you, while countless waters through lands exciting beyond our wildest dreams may one day be paddled by the young and adventurous of many countries.

5

Coastal Touring

CHRIS HARE

To every canoeist the sea presents a challenge sooner or later. For some it is merely a desire to see what is round the headland, or to cross a bay safely, for others it is the crossing of seas and oceans. Sea touring is to the canoeist what mountains are to the rock climber—the culmination of effort, skill and planning—depending, of course, on how severe you wish to make it.

The basic rules and preparation are the same no matter how far you are going, and in the following chapter I will endeavour to explain them. However there is one rule that I learned from the greatest sea kayakers of all, the Greenlanders—make haste slowly. Preparation is the secret of success.

EQUIPMENT

Kayaks

The perfect sea touring kayak has not yet been invented, and variations on the theme are limitless. What is required of the sea touring kayak is a craft that will run on a straight course without being pushed off by a wave; has a low profile so that it is not caught by the wind and blown off course; is capable of being rolled and has good stowage space. However, as most canoeists have only one craft to deal with every type of water, here are some variations to make them more seaworthy:

SLALOM KAYAKS. Being highly rockered they spin round on a following wave and make a journey arduous. However, with the attachment of a skeg (see Fig. 25), or fin, fitting under the craft, the water line is extended and they run a reasonably straight course in the sea.

ESKIMO KAYAKS. Ideal for travelling long distances, but they are usually difficult to store gear in through lack of space.

WHITE WATER RACING CRAFT. A good compromise. Storage space is available and they usually run in a fast straight line. One

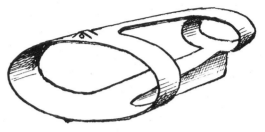

Fig. 25 A skeg

should be careful, however, that the craft of your choice has not a very high bow which makes it prone to catching the wind.

THE GENERAL PURPOSE AND TOURING KAYAKS, although easy to pack, invariably have large cockpits which make it difficult to stay in when rolling the craft. Although the skill of rolling is not essential in the early stages of sea touring, as one becomes more experienced and tackles advanced trips, self rescue in the form of rolling is advantageous to know and practice. Also, spray covers over this type of cockpit have a tendency to leak, so I personally avoid large cockpits.

Rudders
Opinions vary on rudders, and they are very much a matter of personal preference. It is best to have the pedal operated type (see Fig. 26) which makes for easier stowage of gear. They fit ideally to the white water racer and are a definite advantage on this type of craft. The over-stern rudder which swivels up out of the way for launching is the best.

Buoyancy
A kayak must have buoyancy capable of supporting the boat when swamped, and it is a good idea to have buoyancy bags which inflate so that the interior of the kayak, except that round the cockpit area and your equipment, is taken up. Then in the event of a capsize, very little water can enter the boat.

Spray Cover
A good fitting spray cover is essential, preferably one with a quick release strap for easy access to the interior of your craft.

Paddles
These are a very personal thing, and by trial and error you will

know what suits you best. However, you should bear in mind that very large blades tax the strength, and if you are paddling long distances—15 miles or more—then smaller blades will be better. Remember—make haste slowly. The blades themselves can be coloured a fluorescent orange, and these make you more easily sighted by coastguards and so on, as the action of paddling is the same as waving them. A spare pair of paddles should be strapped firmly to the rear deck. For your spare paddles a jointed pair is necessary, but for normal paddling, a rigid shaft is better.

Deck Layout
When paddling at sea everything must be immediately to hand, so I suggest that a series of elastic straps are fixed across the decks of your kayak to hold necessary equipment in place (see Fig. 26).

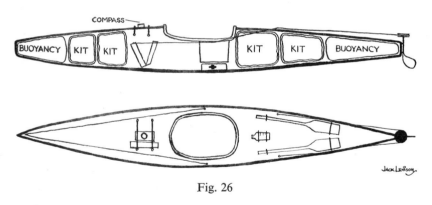

Fig. 26

Repair Kit
Collisions occur at sea, sometimes with rocks, usually with another member of the party, so a repair kit kept by the side of the seat is essential. Sticky tape is a favourite for most types of craft, but remember that you must dry the damaged area first, and you should therefore carry a small towel in the top of your repair kit, or use an ether based liquid such as acetone. (For how to repair see practical training).

Baler
A dinghy baler is very handy for emptying that loaded craft on

which it is difficult to use a rescue method. If you are really fussy use a sponge to finish off the mopping up.

Flares

This is essential emergency equipment, and it is a good idea to have more than one. The Mars Schermully Hand Flare is very good, as is the Pains-Wessex Handstar—a two star flare. I prefer the two star variety which is small and easy to carry in a waterproof cover. Store inside another waterproof bag by the side of the cockpit.

Compass

It is always a good idea to know where you are when the fog comes down; hence the compass. The ideal is a dinghy compass fixed on a gimbal to the deck of your craft. However, this does get in the way during rescues, so an alternative is the Silva oil-filled compass mounted on a board so that it can be slotted under the deck straps.

CLOTHING FOR THE PADDLER

Keeping dry at sea is a problem. Some paddlers try to overcome it by having craft with high freeboard, but these catch the wind. Wetsuits usually restrict movement, unless you have one with no sleeves—these, worn in conjunction with a sweater and anorak, are quite popular. Drysuits make you perspire, and they tear easily. So, an anorak of the specialist type favoured by slalomists, worn with wetsuit trousers and tight sweaters comes out favourite.

Lifejackets and Buoyancy Aids

A lifejacket is a 'must' at sea—it should be worn and not carried in the kayak. There are a number of very good ones on the market, approved by the B.C.U. and B.S.I., but make sure they are roomy around the neck. Chafing in this region can be exceedingly uncomfortable. On the whole avoid buoyancy aids, but personally I like the waistcoat type which pulls on over the head and is filled with strips of foam buoyancy. This helps to keep you warm when paddling and will support you in the water. It will not turn you on to your back if you are unconscious, hence the term 'buoyancy aid' and not 'lifejacket'.

Whistle

A plastic whistle attached to your lifejacket is important for signalling to your companions. Arrange beforehand what the signals will be, and remember that the range of a whistle is limited.

Watch

A waterproof watch of the sub-aqua diver's type is ideal. A knowledge of the time is most important in your distance calculations, tidal stream movement, and so on.

Numbers

Finally, do not go out to sea unless there are three of you, all capable of rescuing each other.

PRACTICAL SEA SKILLS

Paddling over any distance can call upon your reserves of strength, therefore it is necessary for you to be reasonably fit and not to tackle too much at first. Remember you cannot get out and walk home!

At first the sea looks like a mass of undefined water, but on closer examination there are basically four types of wave. A bow wave, a stern wave, a beam wave and a combination of any of these, which will give you a haystack.

BOW WAVES are tackled in relation to their size. Small ones can just be paddled through and ignored. This is what sorts out the sea canoes. If the wave runs up the deck and hits the cockpit, you know the deck is too flat and the bow too shallow. In the steeper type of wave, and this is particularly important in 15-foot boats, paddle into the wave, putting the blade into the oncoming wave just below the top. Over you go, using the back of the blade in a manner similar to a ski stick, and sliding down the back of the wave. This gives a support to the paddler when his boat bounces down and when you crash through a big wave you feel as if the drop is tremendous. The bigger the wave the more determination is needed.

STERN WAVES are basically surfing waves, and the object should be to use them to conserve strength by running forward on the wave, and at sea long distances can be covered with the right technique and conditions. As you are paddling, the kayak will sink into a trough and you are lifted by the following wave. As you are moved forward, paddle until you are on the face of the wave and then run with it. The problem arives when the heavily rockered boats (slalom) then turn off course and have to be corrected with a stern rudder stroke. However, when travelling long distances at sea this will tire you, therefore develop the technique of staying in front of the wave by paddling lightly and keeping on it until the strength of the wave is dispersed. With a 17-foot craft this is usually a relatively simple process as it will usually run very well on even the smallest stern wave. If a rudder is fitted, then you can paddle straight on. It is important to keep the boat at right angles to the oncoming wave. No foot in this world will hold a rudder once the boat has started to run off. After a while cultivate the habit of easing on your paddles in the trough, as here you get the greatest drag on the boat, and you do not go any faster by straining at the paddles. It is extremely rare in deep water for the boat to be 'pooped' by a stern wave (waves swilling over the stern and down the back of your spray cover—Ugh!) In shallow water this often does happen, but does not adversely affect the stability of your craft—in fact it increases it.

The situation does not normally arise whereby you stick your bows in to the extent of looping while in deep water. Although one does sometimes get immersed, but at this point it is a simple matter to stop paddling, and the bows will come out on their own, or by increasing the leverage on the stern rudder stroke, stop the craft moving forward.

BEAM WAVES depend a great deal on their 'hairiness' as to how they are tackled. The roller, or rounded type, can best be negotiated by paddling along the trough, parallel to the wave top. As it overtakes you, sweep stroke the bows round so that the boat is now angled at 45 degrees into the wave top. As the wave overtakes you it will turn you round, and over you go, taking up the bow wave position. With a rudder this works extremely effectively, the only difference being that you do not need the original sweep stroke. When the wave is breaking and you have got the full length of your boat's beam on to it, paddle brace. This is done by sticking the paddle into the wave just under the frothy bit and pulling down on the paddle. The brace will then turn into a high telemark as the boat turns into the wave, and then you go over the top, and skid down the back, using the paddle as a support. With the lower breaking wave a low telemark position so that one leans on top of the wave will give a comfortable ride, and as the power is dispersed then you will swing over the top and glide down the other side (see Fig. 27).

Fig. 27 (a)   Low Brace

Fig. 27 (b)   High Brace

A HAYSTACK is the combination of any two of these waves. This is caused by the wave hitting an obstruction, such as a pier or under-water rocks, rebounding and hitting the following wave. I have been caught by accident or design on a number of these waves, and the result is always the same. Up you go, and invariably come down in the bow wave position with your paddle supporting you. However, this is not the sort of thing to go looking for, and that is why it is important to find out where the snags are, both under water and above, before you set off. For this you need an Admiralty Chart.

In the first instance it is necessary to learn these techniques safely, and where better than on the surfing beach where, when capsizes happen, they are fun and not the first stage of a rescue operation!

Rescue Methods

Now you are competent to paddle about the sea you will realise that the kayak paddler is self-sufficient, and this goes for rescuing himself as well. The ideal form of rescue is, of course, the Eskimo Roll, dealt with elsewhere in this book, but it is as well to have a method of rescue at hand, and the method I prefer is the Rafted 'T' (see Fig. 28).

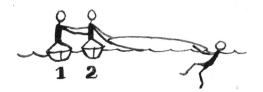

Fig. 28 (i)   No. 1 grips No. 2 firmly around waist, supporting him whilst No. 2 pulls the capsized kayak onto their decks

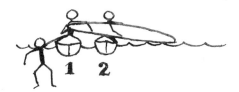

Fig. 28 (ii)   Swimmer goes around to No. 1 whilst 1 and 2 pull upturned kayak onto decks

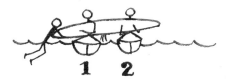

Fig. 28 (iii)   Swimmer pushes down on upturned kayak and with the help of 1 and 2 the water is emptied

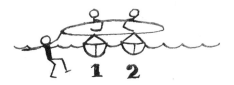

Fig. 28 (iv)   Water is now out. Re-entry should now proceed. Total time: 2 minutes

This method, as can be seen, is very stable, and the strain, which is considerable when dealing with a half-submerged kayak, is put on the decks of two kayaks, and is thereby lessened. The man in the water is called upon to do some work, but not a great deal. This is important, as the fact that he is active does help him to overcome the inherent fear of being in the 'oggin'. Activate his mind, so that he hasn't time to think of getting frightened.

When learning this method, by all means learn in flat calm water, but do not leave it at that. Once competent on flat water, try it in rough or moderately rough seas, under controlled conditions—in a harbour. It is important that you can do a rescue in choppy seas as you rarely capsize in a flat calm!

ESKIMO RESCUES

These rescues are little used among canoeists, and I feel are not practised sufficiently, but their application can save considerable strain on the party. The object is not to leave your capsized kayak, but to wait until another party member comes along and gives you a hand. This is not easy in the wider kayaks of the slalom variety, but in other types it can be done very efficiently indeed, especially if you are wearing the approved type of lifejacket, for it is possible to inflate this with practice, and it will then keep you afloat. It is hard work, and strictly for the expert (see Fig. 29).

Repairs

The collision which brings about the repair at sea often happens during such a rescue as has been described. So take the damaged craft and raft up into the 'T' positions again. The owner disembarks and hangs on to the bows of the raft. Place the damaged boat on the decks of the raft, then carry on with the repair with one of the raft men, or more if there be more, hanging on to the damaged boat while the other dries out the damage and sets to work on the repair. In the case of a heavily loaded craft, unloading and the use of a baler might be necessary first.

THEORETICAL PREPARATION

Charts

I do like to know where I am going, so the easiest way is to get

Fig. 29 (a) Bow Grab method

Fig. 29 (b) Paddle Grab method

a map of the sea and coast—a chart. There is no great mystique about chart reading. They are for the most part self-explanatory. The Admiralty issue two sizes of chart. One which will give you an overall picture of a very large area—up to 40 or 50 miles at a scale of 1 inch to 6.85 miles, or the other, which is really more relevant to the canoeist, of 2 inches to 1 mile. A list of all charts issued with diagrams showing areas, are in the *Catalogue of Admiralty Charts*, 5p from a chart agent.

Now what can we learn from the chart:

DEPTH comes first. A canoe can float in 4 inches of water, but shallow water is very choppy and confused in windy conditions, whereas deep water gives steady wave formations. So on your chart shallow areas, over sandbanks say, are to be approached with caution in certain weather conditions. Depth is shown on a chart in fathoms (6 feet) i.e. $2 = 12$ feet, $2_4 = 2$ fathoms 4 feet; $0_4 = 4$ feet.

DRYING AREAS such as rocks, estuaries, mud flats, reefs are marked, so you can plan your trip to stop at a certain time—when the rocks are dry, or the mud flats covered with water.

SHIPPING CHANNELS AND BUOYS. Important if you are not to be run down, as ships cannot stop, and indeed will not, for the canoeist. So you must know where they are likely to be. The buoys usually mark wrecks, channels and other hazards, and so make signposts on the water for you to find your way by.

ESTUARIES. Where the high and low water mark may mean the difference between landing and launching in comfort, and being up to your knees in mud. Often in estuaries you get large areas of water draining through small river mouths, and it is best not to be there when it starts to ebb out!

OVERFALLS, usually found off headlands, are underwater waterfalls. These are very disturbed areas of sea and best avoided.

HEADLANDS. These invariably have a current or rip on them, and this is recorded in the Pilot Book, or shown on the chart.

REEFS, both underwater and above, will, when the wind is blowing the waves against them, cause haystacks.

CLIFFS AND BEACHES. It is most important to know where there is a possible landing, as from the sea a coastline appears flat and difficult to recognise. It is important to know where you can land —you cannot paddle for ever!

Charts show by their marks the chart datum, which is the minimum level to which the water will fall in that area. So when looking at a chart, try and think in terms of this.

An explanatory chart (No. 5011) giving all the symbols and data used in Admiralty charts is available, and is a first class guide.

PILOT BOOK. In conjunction with your chart, read the Pilot for your area. It will give you a mass of information—not always relevant to the canoeist—but it all helps to build up your picture of the unknown. Finally, you have studied your chart and have a plan in your mind of the route, so do not leave it behind. Waterproof the section you require by covering it with Contact transparent plastic and slip it under your deck straps.

Tides and Tidal Streams

Now that we know a little about the area and the snags that abound, we had better find out a little about what the water is going to do. Firstly, it is a matter of finding out about the tides—

high water and low water—so that you know how deep the water will be and whether the reef marked on the chart $\frac{6}{8}$ (which means drying 6 feet) will in fact be drying or covered when you get there.

TIDES. The tides which are experienced around the coasts of Great Britain and Western Europe are called Semi Diurnal (half daily) which means there are two high waters and two low waters each lunar day (24 hours 50 minutes approximately). About $1\frac{1}{2}$ days after the new moon, or the full moon, the earth, sun, and moon are nearly in line, and the tides produced by the combination of these forces give the highest high waters and the lowest low waters. These are known as Spring tides, and it is then that the tidal streams run at their strongest.

Approximately nine days after the new moon, or the full moon, the lunar and solar forces are acting at right angles to each other, and these conditions create the lowest high waters and the highest low waters, and are called Neap tides, and it is then that the tidal streams run at their slowest.

In the days between Springs and Neaps the height of the tides vary, and the information on their height can best be gained from a set of tide tables from any ships chandlers. The Tide Tables themselves give heights and times for set ports. Should you be in some other area you then use the Tidal Constants System.

The Tidal Constants System gives a set of times and heights which you add or subtract to the time given at a standard port. For instance, in my tide tables you add 1 hour 8 minutes to the time of high tide at London Bridge to get the time of high tide at Queensferry, Scotland.

TIDAL STREAMS. Basically caused by the mass of water flooding from the Atlantic around the shores of Britain and Ireland and back out again. On your chart you will find a capital letter in a diamond referring to information on the chart giving the strength and direction of the tidal stream. In areas where there are islands these streams become complicated and very strong, because of the restriction of the water, so it is important to know when, where and which way they are going. Remember, the canoeist touring travels at some 3 to 4 miles per hour, and if the tidal stream is running at $2\frac{1}{2}$ knots then he will progress extremely slowly if he is travelling against it, and get very tired in the process. More information on this can be gathered from the Pilot book. Do not be fooled into thinking that the turn of the tide is the turn of the tidal stream. In fact, the tidal stream usually turns at half tide.

FINDING YOUR WAY

Once out on the water with your chart, waterproofed and strapped to the deck, it is important that you know exactly where you are and where you are going to be, otherwise harm could come to a young canoeist—or or an old one for that matter. The methods of finding one's way are two-fold: by Transit Bearings, or by Compass.

Transit Bearings consist of taking two prominent landmarks; churches, cranes, chimneys, towers and so on, lining them up and keeping them in line so that you paddle a straight course, avoiding snags (see Fig. 30).

The alternative system is to travel by compass, and it is vitally important that you always carry one and are conversant with its use, as you never know when a fog might catch you unawares, and the sea is a very big pond to get lost in!

Assuming that your compass is fixed to the deck, it is a relatively simple matter to keep the bows pointed in the right direction, and the compass pointing to the course you require.

To get a cross bearing by compass two landmarks as far apart as possible are required. Take a compass bearing on each. Draw them on your chart, and the point at which they intersect marks your position. The big thing about compass work is practice under controlled conditions so that you have faith in your ability to find your way by compass. Then when a fog comes down you can still carry on.

As will have been seen by the foregoing on charts and transits, some knowledge of your speed when paddling is of great help. Obviously there can be no set criterion on speed, but it can be generally said that slalom boats travel at about 4 m.p.h. maximum, white water racers and Eskimo kayaks at 5 m.p.h. maximum. The only way is to keep checking yourself and building up a mental picture of what speed you paddle at normally in relatively easy conditions.

WEATHER

Whether or not, would perhaps be a better definition! The weather is all important at sea, and therefore you should learn all you can of this complex subject. There is no royal road to it, but don't let that deter you. The more you know of weather the more fascinating a subject it becomes.

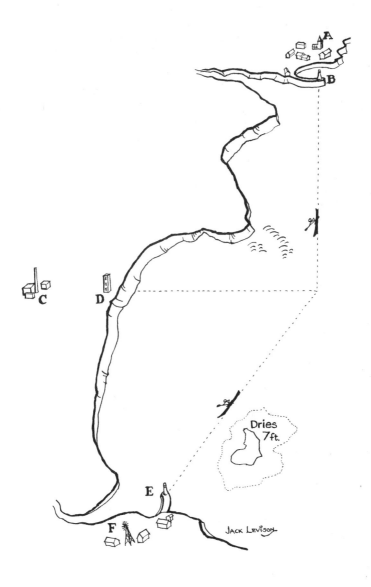

Fig. 30 Using the back bearing A/B the paddler clears the headland and the overfall. When C/D are in line—a cross bearing—he changes course for the transit F/E. This course will carry him clear of the shallow drying area which is a potential hazard in rough conditions

At first one tends to rely on weather forecasts from:

Television	—weather charts
Radio	—shipping forecasts. See *Radio Times*
Telephone	—a weather forecast for your area is always available from the number given in the directory.
Local Weather Centre	—throughout Great Britain there are Local Weather Centres, and they can usually oblige with a more detailed wind forecast than that which is given in the general service put out to the public.
Local aerodromes	—commercial or R.A.F. are usually obliging, especially the R.A.F.
Coastguard	—he will usually give you an accurate forecast of local weather conditions, and it is always handy to ask him when you report your operational area.

So much then for the forecasts that are obtainable. But when it comes to the crunch, it really depends on your judgement and therefore you should be able to foretell the weather with reasonable accuracy yourself. This takes a considerable amount of practice, and it is far too complex a subject to go into in any depth here, but I would recommend that you read *Instant Weather Forecasting* by Alan Watts. This will guide you into learning what causes weather conditions, and more precisely with regard to the canoeist, what causes wind, by reproductions of cloud formations and, as will readily be seen, can be easily applicable to your own situation.

A final thought on weather—winds, to be exact. Try and establish wind speed in relation to trees around your home, or some other normal phenomena, like smoke. This will be a great help to you when a quick estimate is called for.

Wind speeds are governed by the Beaufort Scale, and a canoeist's guide to this is as shown on page 107.

THE TRIP

The preparation is over, the day for *the* trip has arrived. Now, prepared by experience of small bay hopping, the time has come to progress to the first coastal trip. One or two important items must be taken into consideration:

Beaufort Number	General Description	Sea	Canoeists' Criterion
0	Calm	Sea like mirror	Everybody goes out and gets sick! Canadian canoes cross Channel! Surf canoeists commit suicide!
1 1–3 knots	Light air	Ripples appear	Same as for 0, except too rough for Canadians.
2 4–6 knots	Light breeze	Tiny waves. No breaking crests	Same as for 0, except too rough for Canadians.
3 7–10 knots	Gentle breeze	Small waves. Crests begin to form	Life gets interesting for all. Good for practice capsize drill.
4 11–16 knots	Moderate breeze	Medium waves building up. Some white horses	About the limit for the Proficiency Test standard canoeist if on a journey.
5 17–21 knots	Fresh breeze	Decidedly lumpy sea. Many white horses	Anybody over Proficiency standard would enjoy this. On shore usually creates very good surf.
6 22–27 knots	Strong breeze	Large waves everywhere. Continually white horses	Short journeys by Advanced canoeists all right, but you are reaching the border line. Dangerous off-shore.
7 28–33 knots	Near gale	Sea piles up and spindrift off tops of waves	Surf tends to be big on shore. Off-shore, dangerous.
8 34–40 knots	Gale	The difference from a landsman's point of view of these is difficult to say except that the sea looks very lumpy, high breaking waves and spindrift following wind path.	On-shore surf becomes very big, and you spend your time hanging on to your tent.
9 41–47 knots	Strong gale		
10 48–55 knots	Storms		On-shore surf enormous, and you get blown away with your tent.

Time for the trip. Remember you could be pinned down in one spot through bad weather.

The ability of the group, which will number not less than three.

The distance to be travelled each day. You can never accurately judge this. Aim at 15 miles, and be flexible. More some days, less others.

Careful packing is essential. Keep your craft perfectly in trim.

The route will be planned, with emergency landing places in case of trouble. Each member of the party carries a chart; compass directions are written on his deck in waterproof ink.

Rules of the road are virtually non-existent for the canoeist. You keep out of the road of everything while in the shipping channels, and after that it is open house.

ISLANDS AND LANDING. Normally landings on islands are all right, but there are some which are bird sanctuaries, which you are expected to respect. Please do so.

Campsites are usually in sand dunes, so it's open house. But ensure you leave no sign that you have been there. Remember, the canoeist on the sea can travel where no other craft dare go, but don't leave a trail of litter to show where you have been.

You can now truly get way from it all. Travel to places other humans rarely, if ever see, observe wildlife without let or hindrance. The sea is a wonderful friend and a terrible enemy —MAKE HASTE SLOWLY.

6

Slalom

KEN LANGFORD

HISTORY

THE sport of canoe slalom has developed rapidly since it gained international recognition in 1949 when the first World Championships were held on the Rhone in Geneva. The results achieved by the British Team were far from good. However, the enthusiasm generated by this team, and the ideas the team brought back did result in the growth and development of the sport in Britain. Britain sent representatives to the subsequent world championships held every two years. Then, in 1959, at Geneva, Great Britain provided her first world champion in Paul Farrant who was tragically killed in a road accident shortly afterwards. This marked the end of a decade of rapid growth and great advancement in the sport. The retirement of Julian Shaw, Ian Carmichael, and the forced retirement of Keith White due to a shoulder injury deprived Britain of her best paddlers. By 1962, the British Team consisted of paddlers with little international experience but with great enthusiasm. This enthusiasm was to start a new era of growth, beginning with the gaining of bronze medals by the team in the men's kayak singles team event at the 1963 World Championships in Austria, and reaching a climax in the 1967 World Championships at Lipno, Czechoslovakia, where Dave Mitchell, who had been in the 1963 team, gained the silver medal in the kayak singles event. Since 1967 the team as a whole has gained dozens of medals at major international events.

Slalom canoeing is now a popular sport in Great Britain, East and West Europe, the United States, Canada, Japan, Australia and New Zealand. For the past twenty years the Alps have been the metropolis of slalom and been the venue of most of the world championships. The building of an artificial site for the 1972 Olympic Games has set a precedent and may lead to the growth of the sport in countries where rivers would otherwise be unsuitable.

17. The World Championship Slalom course at Bourg St Maurice in France, 1969. An excellent course of very high grade water with many of the boulders placed by contractors to make it one of the best venues in Europe

WHY SLALOM?

Canoe slalom is perhaps the ultimate test of a paddler's ability to apply rough water techniques efficiently to the rough water situation. It is an extremely valuable method of improving an individual's rough water ability safely. It tests the speed at which the paddler can move along a predetermined path. Any mistakes are discovered painlessly because of the substitution of slalom 'gates' for rocks. The competition itself tests to the limit because of the inclusion of the stop-watch. A wrongly placed or inefficient stroke will be indicated in the final times recorded.

It is not, however, in the actual competition that the most learning takes place. How can it be, when both runs total little more than eight minutes? Yet training with gates on rough water is invaluable when perfecting basic rough water techniques. Poles suspended above the water form far safer obstacles than solid rock!

The intending slalomist has two qualities which must be developed separately and which must then be integrated. He must learn to 'read' the water and know what effect it will have on his canoe. He must develop efficient paddle strokes which will enable him to move his craft in the required direction having regard to the force of the water and the speed of the current. The strokes can be learnt initially on flat water but there is no substitute for experience in 'reading' the water and using it to advantage.

EQUIPMENT OF THE SLALOMIST

The Kayak
From 1949 to 1963 all kayaks used at World Slalom Championships were folding. They were generally of rubberised-canvas round an assembled wooden frame. However, the introduction of fibreglass canoes in the early 1960's transformed canoe design and construction. It was realized that a canoe made from glass fibre was an advantage over the canvas canoe. It was often lighter and stronger. After 1963, therefore, the folding kayak singles class, 'F.1', was replaced by the kayak singles class, 'K.1', and open to all types of single seater kayak which had a minimum length of 400 centimetres and minimum beam of 60 centimetres. Inevitably, the folding canoe soon disappeared

from international competition and subsequently from national and regional competition.

The designs of slalom kayaks are numerous. However, three main types exist; Swedish form, fish form, and symmetrical (Fig. 31). There is much to be said in favour of each type, but the fact that all three still exist in large numbers suggests that the choice of kayak is largely one of individual preference.

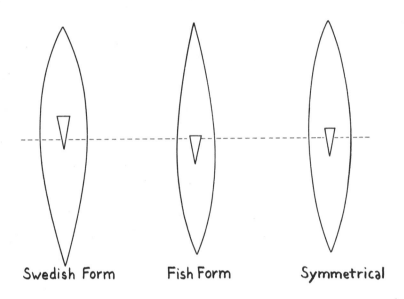

Swedish Form   Fish Form   Symmetrical

Fig. 31   Slalom Kayak designs

Of far greater significance than the basic designs are the fittings of the kayak. The paddler must wear his canoe rather than sit in it; he must be like the classical Greek centaur not the rider on his horse. The paddler must have complete control over the movements of the boat.

Fittings

a. THE SEAT is moulded to fit the average paddler, preventing him from sliding backwards or forwards. It is positioned low in the boat to ensure stability. The paddler's waist should be approximately level with the lip of the cockpit.

b. THE HIP-BOARDS prevent the paddler from sliding from side to side when the kayak is leaned. To be effective they should fit snug against his hips (using padding if necessary).

18. Peter Van Stipdonk of Holland, competing on the River Dee in North Wales at the International Llangollen Canoe Slalom. Here he is taking the first gates on the lower fall

c. THE FOOTREST is adjusted so that the individual can exert pressure with the ball of his foot when paddling.

d. KNEE-GRIPS of some form are essential to give maximum control when the boat is leaned or when the paddler is executing an Eskimo Roli. The position preferred by most people is with the knees about 12 inches apart and with little or no pressure on the knee-caps. Wooden bars are often fitted extending from the front of the coaming to the hip-boards, crossing the thigh just above the knee.

Most manufacturers incorporate these four fittings into the construction of the kayak. Rope loops are fitted to the bow and stern and the kayak is fitted with buoyancy to facilitate easy rescue of the craft in the event of a capsize.

Personal Equipment

a. CRASH HAT is of moulded fibreglass, padded and covering the ears, forehead, top and back of the head, but not rubbing on the paddler's neck. The chinstrap is of non-expanding material to ensure that the helmet remains in position even under pressure of water. The helmet is lightweight and has evenly spaced holes through which water can drain as the paddler does an Eskimo Roll. This prevents a large volume of water trickling down the paddler's face after he has just brought himself upright.

b. THE LIFEJACKET is probably the most widely discussed article of slalom equipment. Controversy rages over when, and when not, to wear one. It is certainly advisable to wear a lifejacket at all times when on moving or open water. In competition it is compulsory and therefore it is best for the paddler to wear it in training. The jacket must contain a minimum buoyancy of 6 kilograms. This is a requirement of both British and international competition. It should also meet the following requirements. It must not restrict breathing or interfere with paddling action. It must be securely fastened so as not to slip off or move up around the paddler's neck if he is in the water. It should be as compact as possible to avoid catching on gates. It should not have too much buoyancy because this will impede Eskimo Rolling. It should be of a padded type all round the body to cushion the impact of rocks when swimming down a rocky river.

c. THE SPRAY COVER consists of a tight apron held over the coaming lip with elastic. To this apron is attached a tube which fits round the paddler's body. It must be tight to allow the water to run off easily and to avoid it collapsing when pounded by heavy waves, and yet it must be possible to release it quickly for safety reasons.

19.   Take off! A competitor at the International Monschau Canoe Slalom in Germany shooting over the boards on the lower fall of the course

The complete paddling equipment of the slalomist is worn in such a way that it allows the least possible amount of water to enter the kayak. A lightweight waterproof anorak over a woollen shirt is adequate for most conditions. However, the weather will determine the amount of clothing worn. The important point is to have the outer garment, in this case the anorak, over the top of the spray cover tube to prevent water running down inside.

All the items of equipment mentioned require regular maintenance. Crash helmet straps become frayed, spray covers leak, elastic snaps. Unless equipment is maintained it will lose its effectiveness.

The Paddles

The paddle blades are set at right angles to each other, referred to as 'feathering'. This facilitates Eskimo Rolling and also gives a far smoother paddling action. There is an increasing tendency to have an oval paddle shaft, particularly for the control hand, which enables the paddler to feel the position of the blade without having to look at it.

Generally, curved blades are used. This has the same effect as a slight cupping of the hand in front crawl swimming. It allows for an easier entry and a more powerful stroke, and as slalom events are about 95 per cent forward, paddling forward speed is very important. The paddle is about 210 centimetres long and a good one weighs less than 3 pounds.

Several types of paddle are available on the market at varying prices. It is true to say that in buying one you get what you pay for. A cheap paddle will not last as well as an expensive one. Basically, the paddler must familiarize himself with all the various types of slalom paddle and then buy whichever comes within his budget, remembering that 'cheap' is not synonymous with 'economic' and that the more expensive paddle is both more durable and also is generally more efficient in use.

BASIC PADDLING STROKE

The paddler adopts the body position shown in Fig 32. All movements he makes start from the hips. The paddles are held at slightly more than shoulder width apart. The exact distance varies with the individual.

Stroke Cycle

a. Start with the left arm extended and left shoulder forward (Fig. 32), right elbow bent at 90 degrees and right blade leaving the water, eyes looking straight ahead, back straight and leaning slightly forward.

b. Raise right wrist to shoulder level, elbow kept low, right shoulder raised.

c. The left arm is kept straight and lowered to allow the left blade to enter the water as far as possible and against the side of the boat.

d. The right arm is then pushed straight forward followed by a rotation of the trunk allowing the right shoulder to follow through as the left arm bends and pulls the left blade to level with the body. (The left arm is now at 90 degrees).

e. Raise left wrist. . . . (Repeat from 'b').

Throughout the stroke cycle a firm hold is maintained by one hand, allowing the other to slip through 90 degrees between the 'pull' and 'push' phases of the 'slip-hand'. The stroke cycle is both regular and continuous, with the paddle pivoting round an imaginary point approximately 18 inches in front of the paddler's chest and 4 to 6 inches above the deck of the kayak. (These distances again vary according to the individual and the type of kayak).

Back paddling is almost a reverse of the forward paddling technique, with the following points being most significant.

a. In order to line up accurately for a reverse gate, the paddler looks over one shoulder only.

b. The paddle enters the water against the boat, pressing flat down on to the surface of the water. This increases the stability of the boat. As the right blade is pressed down on to the water, the left hand is pulled over the paddler's head.

c. The back of the blade is used for reverse paddling.

Fig. 32 Basic paddling stroke—arm straight—eyes looking forward

SLALOM TECHNIQUE

Before 1956 little consideration was given to the effectiveness of specific slalom strokes. Paddlers relied on balance for stability, and on a flailing windmill action of the paddles for propulsion. Then, in 1956, Zigi Holzbauer, a German, introduced the techniques of Emile Duffek to Britain. Duffek was a Czech refugee who late became a naturalized Swiss. His contribution to slalom was in adapting Canadian-canoe paddling techniques for use in a kayak with the extra blade waving above the paddler's head (Fig. 33). Although considered at one time to be unecessarily exhibitionist in character, the Duffek strokes form the basis of present-day kayak slaloming. The paddle became an instrument of stability as much as balance had been prior to this time.

Strokes can be divided into distinct categories, although it is the adaption of the strokes into an effective sequence which distinguishes the better from the poorer paddlers.

The composition of a 'stroke sequence' will determine the route of the kayak. These are positive strokes. If the path taken by the kayak determines the stroke sequence, these are correction strokes. In slalom, a correction stroke is negative and does not normally aid propulsion. It is therefore expensive in both time and effort and should be avoided as much as possible. The paddler, therefore, must know the effect of a stroke before he actually performs it. This is largely a matter of individual experience. However, there are certain basic strokes which are fundamental to slalom technique. The paddler adapts a stroke, or series of strokes, to the situation as he expects to find it. This infers thought and planning before the situation is encountered.

The Draw Stroke
The paddle is held in the normal paddling position. The wrists are dropped to allow the blade to enter the water parallel to the kayak, with the arms fully extended and the paddler looking at the blade. The paddle is then pulled towards the boat with the top arm remaining fairly straight (Fig. 33). The boat is drawn towards the paddle. The blade is then turned through 90 degrees by flexing the wrist and sliced through the water to the starting position with both arms again extended.

Throughout the stroke the boat remains on an even keel to enable it to move sideways more easily. It has the greatest effect when the boat is stationary and is, therefore, of limited use in slalom.

Turning
To be able to turn the kayak with the minimum expenditure of time, effort and speed loss is a basic requirement of the slalom course. The most common method of turning is by the use of the 'telemark'. This necessitates leaning the kayak and support-

ing the individual's weight on the paddle. The two different telemark turns perform quite separate functions and it is therefore necessary to select the correct one for a particular situation.

Fig. 33 Draw Stroke—kayak remains on even keel, paddle almost vertical

The High Telemark Turn

The paddle is held in the same position as for forward paddling with the arms stretched out in front. The wrists are then raised and the elbows dropped, allowing the blades to turn through 180 degrees so that the face of the blade is presented to the surface of the water. The paddler keeps his back straight and leans forward slightly.

The paddle is placed in the water at an angle of between 30 and 70 degrees to the water. It is then held with the face of the blade pointing towards the bow of the kayak. The 'rudder' effect of the paddle blade will cause the boat to pivot round the paddle, and, if at the end of the turn the paddle blade is pushed towards the bow of the kayak, the boat will be drawn towards the paddle, giving an even smaller turning circle. Throughout the turn the kayak is leaned. This shortens the effective length of the kayak and increases the 'rocker' of the boat, so facilitating easier turning.

Fig. 34   High Telemark Turn—kayak is leaned, paddle almost vertical

The Bow Rudder Stroke

This is a variation of the high telemark and is used when a slight directional change is required without loss of speed. The paddle is placed in the water in the high telemark position, but with the blade as far forward as possible, and then held until the required directional change has been achieved. The stroke is normally followed by a forward paddle stroke on the same side, without the paddle actually leaving the water.

The Low Telemark Turn

The paddle is held in the normal paddling position. The elbows and shoulders are then raised and the wrists dropped presenting the back of the blade to the surface of the water. The paddle is pressed downwards and away from the boat. The effect is to push the boat away from the paddle. The action of pressing down on the water results in a slight lifting of the stern which further helps turning.

From the explanation of the two distinct telemark turns it is evident that each serves a different function. The high telemark is most suited for cutting out of a fast current by pulling the kayak into the slack water. The boat is turned mainly from the bows as they reach the slack. The paddle remains fairly stationary as the boat revolves round it. The opposite is the case with the low telemark. The stroke is therefore used when changing direction in fast water. The stern is lifted on the initial 'push' of the stroke, making this the fastest of the turns used in slalom.

Fig. 35   Low Telemark Turn—kayak is leaned

The Forward Sweep Stroke

The paddle is held in the normal paddling position. The right hand is brought into the chest, without changing the grip on the paddle. The left hand is fairly straight. The body is then rotated clockwise to allow the left hand to reach farther forward. The left blade enters the water and with the left arm remaining straight, describes a semi-circle while the body rotates anti-clockwise from the hips. The left hand describes as large an arc as possible, the kayak leaning slightly on the paddling side to increase the turning effect. Stability is maintained by the action of the paddle on the water, the face of the blade pointing slightly downwards.

This stroke is extremely useful for slalom in that it enables a change in direction to be accomplished while still propelling the kayak forward. For this reason it often replaces the bow rudder stroke, except when control is required over the stern section of the kayak. The effect of the sweep stroke is more a change of direction by pivoting the kayak round the paddler's body, whereas the bow rudder tends to draw the whole boat sideways. The sweep stroke is often used to begin a directional change or push the kayak towards slack water, prior to executing a telemark turn.

20. The Telemark turn. Note the reversed left wrist, the pressure the canoeist is exerting with his right hand, the way he is looking behind him, and the speed with which the stern is scudding sideways across the surface. Note, above all, the complete confidence the canoeist has in leaning his whole weight on his paddle blade

All the strokes mentioned so far can be considered positive. They provide the required propulsion and stability needed for the slalom course. However, when a mistake or error of judgement is made it may be necessary to perform a correction stroke to restore stability. Three movements fall within this category, and, while not strictly slalom strokes, they are vital to the slalomist in that the degree of perfection in them will minimize or exaggerate the time-loss caused by the original mistake. In each case the movements involve no change in the gripping of the paddle.

The Slap Support Stroke

The need for this stroke generally arises when a change of current exerts pressure against one side of the kayak, causing it to capsize on the upstream side. If the paddler reacts quickly, he can prevent the capsize by means of a slap support. He raises both elbows, allowing the forearms to become vertical, and then presses hard or slaps the water with the back of the blade forcing the canoe upright again.

Fig. 36   Slap Support Stroke—elbows high, paddle horizontal

Hanging Support Stroke

If the slap support fails and the canoe is still being capsized by the force of the water, the paddler can allow his elbows to drop,

Fig. 37   Hanging Support Stroke—elbows down, paddle as horizontal as possible

causing the blade to turn through 180 degrees with the result that he hangs from the paddle which is still as near horizontal as possible. The paddler performs the same action of correcting the boat by pulling hard on the paddle, bringing him upright again.

The effect of both these strokes can be increased or sustained by a sculling action backwards and forwards along the surface of the water. This would be necessary if the paddler was held broadside in a 'stopper' where it would be necessary to lean downstream deliberately to counteract the force of the water and to ensure that the upstream gunwale of the canoe remains clear of the water.

The Eskimo Roll

If the two support strokes mentioned have failed, the paddler will have to effect an Eskimo Roll or else bale out of the kayak. A roll will allow him to continue his run, whereas a bale-out will not. It is therefore essential to be able to do an Eskimo Roll if the occasion should demand it. There are several different types of roll, each with its own teaching progressions; Pawlata, Steyr, Put-across, etc. However, for slalom the most useful is the Screw Roll. This is a development of the hanging support stroke but includes a twist of the body to make the roll possible.

For a roll to be useful in slalom it must satisfy the following requirements. There should be no need to change the position of the hands on the paddle. Doing so would possibly lead to the loss of the paddle, particularly in rough water. It would certainly lead to an unstable position when the roll is completed and would waste valuable time. The paddler should be able to lean forward when upside down in order to protect himself. This is often instinctive; just as a hedgehog will curl into a ball to protect the vital organs of the body, so the paddler must lean forward to protect his face when floating upside down along a rocky river bed.

This is why the Screw Roll is recommended for slalom. If a roll becomes necessary on the slalom course, it is to the individual's advantage to use the current which capsized him in order to roll up. This means that he should be able to roll equally well on both sides in order to effect a 360 degree roll.

The Slalom Course

In looking at the effects of tidal waves, storms, and floods it is realized that water is an extremely powerful and damaging force when not controlled. In its natural state it cannot be defeated by man, and certainly not by one individual in a slalom kayak. An inspection of damage caused by a river in flood is sufficient to point out the futility of working against the water. The river is reluctant to give second chances to anyone who underestimates its power, and a twenty kilo boat is broken just as easily as a nine kilo one!

It is this type of water which attracts the slalomist. A course will consist of a half mile section of river, with waves, eddies, conflicting currents, and fast flowing water throughout its length. It may consist of the agitated water at the foot of a weir, particularly the Thames weirs.

The aim of the slalom course is to test the paddler's ability to handle his craft and execute the principal strokes, turns, break-outs, and so on, which he might reasonably be expected to encounter while touring on a rapid river. It also tests his initiative in using the power of the water to his own advantage, without letting the water take advantage of him. To do this he must be able to 'read' and interpret accurately the characteristics of the river. The effects of changes in current must be studied closely. They will determine such factors as which way to approach a gate or which way to turn between gates.

A slalom course provides two extremes in water conditions:

a. BLACK WATER. Generally smooth and constant in its flow, therefore containing few air bubbles and having a black or grey-black appearance. This type of water, when moving fast, is the most powerful.

b. WHITE WATER. Turbulent and agitated, containing a large amount of air, giving it a white or milky appearance, and having a fluctuating surface level. It is far less buoyant and the kayak will sit lower in the water.

Down the length of the course, between 15 and 30 gates will be positioned. The majority of these will be negotiated forwards downstream but there will be three or four gates which must either be negotiated in reverse or forwards upstream. Each gate will be at least four feet wide, and as the paddler goes through it, the red and white pole will be to his left and the green and white pole to his right. The competitor is timed from the start to the finish and penalties are added to his time for each gate nego-tiated incorrectly. His total penalty points are added to his elapsed time to give a final total, recorded in seconds. The paddler has two attempts at the course, the best one counting in the competition.

As each competitor only has one practice run on the course before the event, it is essential that his slalom technique and his ability to read the water allow him to make the best of that run.

Learning to Read Rough Water

In the early stages of river canoeing, much can be learnt from studying the river from the bank. Most rapids in England can be canoed successfully by the novice paddler. The problems arise when things happen so fast that he has no time to appreciate the situation in which he has put himself, and to do the appropriate stroke to prevent a capsize. Yet with careful planning of the strokes he intends to use he can work out from the bank which channel to take, which way to lean his boat, and what strokes to use. Once he has canoed the section he can then assess for himself just how accurate was his reading of the water.

Two points have now arisen which accompany any shooting of rapids. Firstly, the planning, the assessment of the rapid, the choice of channel; and secondly, the post-mortem following the attempt. The post-mortem is the most vital part if anything is to be learnt and if progress is to be made. Was each stroke successful? Was any stroke unnecessary? Did the chosen channel prove to be the right one? If in doubt, is it worth trying again?

This then is the crux of all rough water paddling. Reading rough water is an art based on experience which has been consolidated over a period of time. A top slalomist knows whether he can do a particular gate sequence just by watching from the bank. He is looking for ways to save what may be a fraction of a second. The novice will, perhaps, be looking to see how he can save himself the price of a new boat! At all levels, inspection from the bank is of great importance.

The techniques necessary to cope with rough water can be learnt much more quickly if a planned approach is adopted. The swimming pool is obviously an ideal place to develop confidence in a 'white water' or slalom canoe. Yet it also provides a starting point for learning the rough water techniques that are so important to slalom. Support strokes, Eskimo Rolling, and so on, can be introduced in the pool before trying them in the real situation of a rapid river. Yet it is only on the river that the paddler finds out whether his aesthetic high telemark actually pulls him into a 'break-out', or whether his Eskimo Rolling is as effective in a cold river as in the heated swimming pool. Training with a stop-watch will indicate the effectiveness of his techniques over a period of time, and regular competition will give him the incentive to improve.

SLALOM IN BRITAIN

Slalom in Britain is organized into four divisions, Division One at the top, and then Divisions Two, Three, and Novices. Each competitior must be a member of the British Canoe Union and can receive details of all events held in the year. By achieving a good result in competition, he is promoted to the next higher division until he eventually reaches the First Division. At the end of each year, the poorer paddlers in a division are demoted to allow for the promotion of better paddlers to that division. The National Champion is chosen from Division One, and is the individual who achieves the best results in three out of five of the First Division Competitions in a year. Slalom in Britain is a fast growing sport with classes for Men's Kayak Singles, Ladies' Kayak Singles, Men's Canadian Singles, and Men's Canadian Doubles. The most hotly contested class both in Britain and in World Championships is Men's Kayak. However, the Canadian canoes have developed rapidly in Britain in the last four years.

Slalom canoeing is a sport which can give a tremendous amount of satisfaction. Whether it is the competition against others or simply the challenge of rough water is immaterial. It is a sport which has been rapidly expanding for some twenty years and there seems no reason why it should not continue to do so.

21. British paddlers Jon Goodwin and John Court competing at Llangollen in the International Canoe Slalom

7

Racing: Sprint and Long Distance

MARIANNE WILSON

THE two main branches in racing are sprint and long distance. Sprint is an Olympic event which was introduced into the Games in 1936 and is staged over set distances of 500, 1,000 and 10,000 metres, under the auspices of the International Canoe Federation. In Great Britain it is controlled by the Paddling Racing Committee of the British Canoe Union who are affiliated to the ICF. Long distance racing is a very popular pastime in this country but does not attract the same interest abroad; the main exceptions being the Sella River Race in Spain, the Danish Gudena 117 kilometre race, and isolated events in Australia and America which bear little resemblance to long distance racing as we know it. It, too, is controlled by a Committee of the BCU. Courses can range in distance from 8 to 124 miles, the latter being the famous Devizes to Westminster Canoe Race inaugurated in 1949 and considered in some quarters as the forerunner to long distance racing as it is known today.

SPRINT RACING

Sprint racing may be considered the purest form of canoeing since it is a competition of speed in matched boats on static, or near static water. The word 'sprinting' is very misleading as medically and theoretically any event over 10 seconds in duration is no longer classed as a sprint, whereas canoe sprinting over the shortest official distance of 500 metres takes approximately 1 minute 50 seconds for a world-class man and 2 minutes 3 seconds for a world-class woman. Therefore, the word 'sprinting' is used in the broadest sense.

The starts in sprint are static and over 500 and 1,000 metres. The course is straight and buoyed, with the competitors being not less than five metres apart and not more than nine in number in any race. The water must have a minimum depth of six feet over the entire course so that no one competitor has unfair advantage over another. These racing conditions have hitherto been virtually unknown in Great Britain but, with the opening of the National Watersports Centre at Holme Pierrepont, Nottingham giving a 2,000 metre course suitable for rowing and canoeing and a similar course proposed for the Lea Valley area, London, British sprint canoeists are now getting the opportunity of racing on a course laid out to international specifications.

The boats used in sprint racing are kayaks and Canadians. Dealing with the kayak first, the single is recognized by the notation K1 for a single, K2 for a double, and K4 for a kayak seating four persons. K-class boats are constructed of either hot moulded veneer, or materials such as fibreglass, and other modern fibres, on the monocoque principle, i.e. frameless and without a keel. They are beautiful craft, sleek, but due to the design, rather unstable. The dimensional and weight limits are governed by the ICF and must conform to the following table given in metric units:

Type	Max. Length	Min. Beam	Min. Weight
	(in centimetres)		(in kilograms)
K1	520	51	12
K2	650	55	18
K4	1100	60	30
C1	520	75	16
C2	650	75	20

As the subject of design is amply covered by Mr Samson in Chapter 9, I do not propose to dwell on it any further.

Canadian sprint racing is virtually non-existent in Britain. The last time we had a competitor in the Olympic Games was in 1952, when Gerald Marchand of Richmond Canoe Club represented Great Britain at Helsinki. However, this type of racing is extremely popular in other countries.

Paddles

There are two basic shapes available to paddlers, either the orthodox 'square' blade or the asymmetrical blade. Both are feathered to decrease wind resistance to the absolute minimum, and light, and manufactured with racing in mind—therefore, they will not stand up to too much harsh treatment.

It has been felt for a considerable time that there is room for

a great deal of research into paddles. The asymmetrical shape was introduced initially by continental manufacturers, and experiments have shown that when the conventional blade enters the water the resistance is off centre and the blade has a tendency to twist, whereas with the asymmetrical shape the centre of pressure remains on the centre of the blade at all points of entry. Some work has been done on paddles in this country and findings indicate that it may be reasonable to expect that an efficient paddle will probably have most of the following features:
1. A laminated construction
2. Curved in a longitudinal direction
3. A shaped centre rib on front surface to give blade stability
4. An asymmetrical shape.

A recent innovation by a British manufacturer has been the use of a special fibreglass cloth forming a tubular shaft giving exceptional strength and flexibility with minimum weight. Also, this paddle incorporates a special handgrip for the controlling hand. It is considered by many canoeists to be a considerable improvement on the conventional wooden laminated loom.

The length of the paddle is decided initially by standing, barefooted, with feet together and the paddle, with one end on the ground, held vertically in front of you. Stretch one arm fully in an upward direction and just curl the tips of the fingers over the top of the blade. I say, initially, as often once a paddler has become experienced he likes to experiment with different lengths until ultimately the ideal length for him is found. The width of grip on the loom is also very important and again, can be found by standing with paddle held horizontally in front of you with your hands on the loom so that you have a right angle at your elbow and also between your upper arm and the sides of your trunk. This gives the correct spacing for your hands. Some people use the same method but place the paddle on their heads. It has been found that if a piece of tape is put on the inside and outer limits of the grip it helps in keeping the hands in the right position when paddling. It is surprising how often you see a canoeist holding the paddles unevenly, the hands having slipped either to right or left.

Training to become a Sprint Paddler
To become a top-class paddler you need a K1 in good condition, suitable paddles, a good technique and the right approach. The

most important thing, in my opinion, is the right approach! You must want to win and mean to work hard enough to achieve this end. Positive thinking is the key and without it you might as well forget the idea of racing successfully. A good K1, the right paddles, and a good technique will get you so far but after that it is all in the mind. Having to train in adverse weather conditions, having to push past the point where your muscles are crying out for you to stop, having to stick to a disciplined routine—this is where your mind must take over and push you through.

22. Sprint racing—Women's K1 singles off the start of a 500 m event

Let us assume that you have the right mental approach and have obtained the K1 and paddles. The next essential is a good basic technique. The following method has not been devised by me but by continental coaches with years of practical experience behind them, and is now widely taught to beginners with great success. Of course, this is not the only technique in current use, and no two people appear to paddle the same as they all have natural limitations and characteristics but the aim of all styles must be to prove as mechanically efficient in the water as possible, and it is up to the paddler and coach to try to achieve this end.

Technique

The basic principle of this technique is that the stroke does not start in the shoulders, but in the hips. The movement runs from the hip muscles over the back and chest to the shoulders and on to the upper forearm. The bodywork is supported by corresponding legwork, the opposite leg to the pushing hand being stretched in rhythm with the stroke, the foot pressed against the footrest. This movement is widely known as the 'cycling' action of the legs.

Sit upright, or lean very slightly forward in the boat, not too far or this will impede abdominal movement and breathing, and do not look into the cockpit or to the bow as this will tend to endanger the straight running of the boat. Look in the direction in which you are travelling. The legs are bent with closed knees and the steering bar held between the feet with the balls of the feet placed on the footbar and the heels resting together on the floor of the boat. Do not press the knees against the sides of the canoe, which is a common and erroneous method when first paddling a K-class boat, as it gives a false sense of stability. In fact, the legs cannot be used correctly and the transfer of effort through the knees into the cockpit will have a tipping effect on the boat.

To describe the movement of the paddle through air and water I will work systematically by giving the stroke on one side of the body. The work of the body starts by moving the hip forward, i.e. in the direction of the first stroke. Simultaneously with this movement, the hand brings the paddle forward at eye level, the back of the hand forming one line with the forearm (wrist straight), and in a straight line in the direction of the gunwale. Do not move the hand in the direction of the centre line of the boat, or across it, as this will upset the smooth running of the craft, which is all-important. The less dipping and rolling movements transferred to the boat the smoother and, therefore, faster it will travel. During the pushing phase of the movement the loom of the paddle is not gripped too

23. Sprint racing—K4 crews, competing at the World Championships of 1970 held in Denmark, turn one of the buoys on the 10,000 m course. The crews are British on the right, and Polish on the left, with the crew from the USA coming up behind

tightly but rather sits in the crutch between the thumb and fore-finger with the fingers extended. Similarly, during the pulling phase the loom is gripped firmly to prevent water slipping away from the blade area and to transfer the power. This 'milking' action of gripping and relaxing the fingers allows fresh oxygen and blood to get to the muscles, which is essential, otherwise the cramped action of holding the muscles static for a period of time will, in due course, lead to strained forearm muscles and possibly to Teno-Synovitis, a common complaint to beginners.

When the arm is straight and the trunk fully rotated, bring the forward hand with the paddle straight down. Just before the blade dips into the water, turn it by a quick 90 degree flick of the wrist of the other hand, i.e. feather the blade to present it vertically to the water. Now we have come to the most im-portant part of the whole movement—the pulling phase. Make certain that the arm is straight and the body is still fully rotated in a forward direction, then the blade must be dipped smoothly into the water just outside the wave which runs from bow to stern. If the paddle enters too closely to the boat, the paddle tends to curve in the first and last quarter of the stroke which causes the craft to veer off course resulting in a loss of speed. The first third of the stroke when the blade enters the water, and is pulled in a straight line backwards through the vertical position, is the most important part so it is essential that the blade is introduced into the water as far forward of the cockpit as possible. It is then carried backwards with a powerful pulling movement from the hip and shoulder muscles. The stroke ends level with the hip. After it has passed this point the blade is in an inefficient position mechanically and also has a braking effect on the speed of the boat.

The lifting of the blade from the water is effected by the other side of the body being rotated, keeping the arm straight and shoulder dropped in preparation for the commencement of the pulling phase on that side. The length of time spent with the blade out of the water must be kept to an absolute mini-mum as no propulsive effort can be applied (Figs. 38 & 39).

Training Schedule

The next step is to adopt an efficient training schedule for the year. This is broken down into three interlinked periods, namely, winter training, pre-racing training, racing training.

Keep an accurate record at all times of the work you have

done, how you feel, morning pulse rate, weight, results and times achieved, etc. This can be a very useful guide in the future as to what sort of training achieves the best results, what period is necessary for obtaining peak condition, how you have progressed over the year, and can also convey a great deal of relevant information to a coach or doctor. The morning pulse rate should be taken before doing anything else. Keep a watch

Fig. 38 The paddle cycle

by the side of the bed. The pulse rate will indicate your state of fitness as the lower it is the fitter you are becoming, or can indicate by a sudden rise an approaching illness, or that you are overdoing training. A loss in weight can indicate that the training is too harsh as well, especially if it is a sudden drop in weight, or it could suggest that a medical check-up is advisable. Obviously, everybody has a gradual loss in weight during the paddling season but most people find that this levels off at their 'racing weight'. Many paddlers like to have a medical check-up at the beginning of the season and I think it is a good idea as it gives you a psychological up-lift when the doctor passes you A1. He might suggest certain vitamins for you to take during an intensive schedule such as Vitamins E and C, and an iron supplement can be added to the diet.

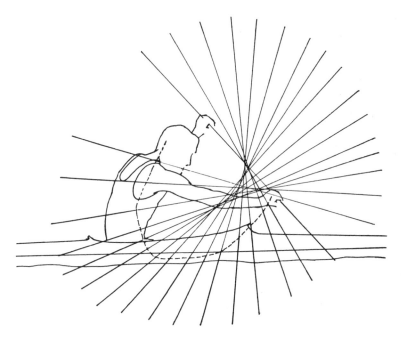

Fig. 39 Superimposed outline of the paddle cycle. The broken line indicates the path of the hand during the 'pulling' phase of the stroke

To understand your training and why you do certain things it is as well to have a basic knowledge of how your body works. As canoeists, our primary concern is the conditioning to maximum efficiency of the trunk rotators, shoulder and arm muscles. A simple outline of muscle physiology and its relationship to the other body systems may help in understanding how this end is achieved; you should study one of the numerous books which have been written on this subject.

WINTER TRAINING—OCTOBER TO MARCH

General fitness can be obtained by running, swimming, games, gymnastics, free-standing exercises, etc. Running improves your cardio-vascular system and the coronary circulation improves enormously which is very important to alleviate coronary thrombosis in later life. If training is done for a long time the heart, in fact, enlarges and it is not a bad thing to have an enlarged heart. Providing there is no disease in the heart it is almost impossible to damage it. When running it is not a case of just going out and jogging along; one must work hard at it as you would at weight training, or paddling. One schedule that is advocated to start at the beginning of December should consist of the following, five nights a week:

$\frac{1}{4}$ mile run slowly—followed by—100 yards flat out
followed by $\frac{1}{4}$ mile fast x 8.

This to be terminated at the end of March followed by one such session per week. Running up hills interspersed with suitable exercises is favoured by some; if available, sand dune running is excellent. But it is a fact that running is an extremely important part of winter training and it should be *hard* running.

Swimming can be performed one night per week as this helps to relax the muscles. The session should consist of hard varied swimming and not just fooling around in the water. Concentrate on front crawl, back crawl and butterfly, as these three strokes use similar muscles to canoeing. Try to have a game of football, basketball or volleyball once a week. Gymnastics are excellent but here the skill level could be the limiting factor. Free-standing exercises help to loosen up the body and are valuable in getting the body warmed through before attempting weight or circuit training, or even paddling on a cold day. On the continent, skiing is an important part of winter training as the downward thrust has marked similarity to the pulling phase of the canoeing stroke. However, except in Scotland, there are few British paddlers who have a chance of enjoying this pastime.

Introduce as much variation as possible into your winter training. There is plenty of enforced routine training in the summer when it is difficult to introduce a lot of variety but in the winter there are many ways of getting fit that are good fun as well.

Once basic fitness has been obtained you should progress to training at a more intensive level, and it is now accepted that the use of weights is a most valuable part of an athlete's training. It was first introduced in 1936 by the Germans who used it in the preparation of their Olympic team.

Strength and power are best obtained by using heavy weights with low repetitions and endurance and stamina is best obtained by using light weights, or body weight, with a high number of repetitions. An ideal schedule is to start with weight training and then progress to circuit training.

Strength is the ability to produce force, and power is the ability to produce force continually. You must work at maximal, or near maximal, level to improve strength with few repetitions.

The generally accepted number of days per week for weight training is three, i.e. Monday, Wednesday and Friday. Sessions should be arranged so that you have a day's recovery in between. You may find at first that you feel very stiff on days following training but if there is no actual injury then there is no reason to miss a session.

Keep a log of your progress, recording at each session exactly what you have done—this will give you the necessary information for the next session. Do not rely on your memory as it is unlikely that you will be able to remember the poundage used for each exercise and your log will also show you how you are progressing and give you information as to when you should change or adjust your schedule.

If you are a beginner, you would be well advised to join a weightlifting club where you can get expert guidance and also have the use of good apparatus, or at least train with people who have more experience than yourself. Never try to lift heavy weights by yourself, otherwise, if you get into difficulties, there is nobody to help you. I remember once becoming caught under the bar whilst doing Bench Press and I had to yell the house down before anybody came to my aid, and I realized what a silly thing I had done. Technique is an integral part of weight training and this is something that cannot be learnt efficiently from books: you have to be shown and coached.

The racing canoeist uses the upper body and trunk, therefore a schedule should be devised that caters mainly for these muscles. The legs are not so important and they are covered

24. Long distance racing—trouble for a crew on the International Liffey Descent course in Ireland. The shoot of such a weir should be made sideways over the sill only, in both K2 or K1. Recovery from such a position is doubtful—this crew are certainly out of the race as their kayak can be seen to be breaking up just to the rear of the front cockpit!

to some extent by running. From the following list of exercises a schedule can be built up:

Squats
Bench Press
Straight Arm Pullovers
Upright Rowing
Bent-over Rowing
Rotation Sit-ups
Lateral Raise
Military Press
Wrist Rolling
Single Arm Rowing

There are other exercises which can be incorporated but the ones mentioned above are the ones most widely used by canoeists. When working out a schedule, take six exercises and arrange them so that you are not using the same muscle groups consecutively. For instance, Bench Press, Straight Arm Pullover, Rotation Sit-ups, Wrist Rolling—these exercises are not using the same muscles.

At the beginning of the strength training season have an introductory period of two to three weeks, assuming training is being done on three evenings per week. Relatively light weights will be used at first and attention can be given to technique. Working poundages must be assessed initially by trial and error; if the poundage is correct you will only just be able to complete the last repetition in your final set. If this cannot be achieved the weight is too heavy, and if it can be achieved too easily the weight is too light.

As with all methods of training there are various ideas on how a schedule should be constructed and I will mention several methods.

(a) Three sets of six repetitions. After each set you should have a reasonable rest. If you are training in a group of three, do the exercises in strict rotation and you will find that this gives ample rest.

(b) Four sets of three repetitions in each exercise.

(c) Five sets of two repetitions in each exercise. A suggested progression from this would be:

(d) A pyramid set consisting of four, three, two and one repetition in each exercise.

(e) A pyramid set consisting of eight, six, four repetitions at one weight, say 75 pounds, and then three, two, one repetitions starting at three at 70 pounds, then two at 75 pounds, and finally one at 80 pounds.

An experienced weightlifting coach will be able to gauge your abilities and will suggest what method to adopt.

Once you are able to do one more repetition after what should be your last repetition, the working poundage should be increased. Generally speaking, the larger the muscle groups which are being used, the greater will be the increase. As the weights get heavier you will need a longer recovery period between each set.

It has been suggested that the introduction of 'Olympic' lifts into a weight training programme will be an asset in the development of power. However, because of the speed of the movement a greater degree of technique is required with these exercises:

Power Cleans
Clean and Jerk
Power Squats
Snatching

But a word of warning—these lifts should be attempted only with experienced lifters.

Paddling at this period of training takes a minor role. Some top paddlers do not paddle at all and, if the winter is a severe one, many stretches of water are iced over. However, if you can get on the water this is a very good time to concentrate on your technique, correcting any faults, and also to build up paddling mileage. Always try to paddle in a group just in case you get into trouble or capsize. Wear suitable clothing—there is no need to go out bundled up but rather wear a long-sleeved woollen jumper, an anorak which is windproof and a tracksuit. If you have particular trouble with cold legs a pair of wetsuit trousers helps to keep you warm and I have found that wetsuit bootees have solved the problem of cold feet. With the use of a spray deck you should be very warm. Unfortunately, your hands will suffer with the cold. You can rub the backs with grease, making sure you do not get it on the inside of your hands, but do not wear gloves. Actually, your warming-up exercises before getting on to the water will help to warm them up.

PRE-SEASON TRAINING: MARCH TO MAY

At the end of February a circuit can be introduced on the second evening of weight training so that you would be doing a weight session, a circuit and another weight session. As I mentioned earlier there must be a progression throughout your whole year's training cultimating in actual racing.

Circuit training, where you have a high number of repetitions and low weights, or body weight, will not make you as strong as weight training but it will improve endurance. It improves both the circulation and the efficiency of the muscles to contend with extended exercise. You may have heard the expression, 'local endurance': this means that the muscle groups used in paddling must be trained in such a way that they can work for long periods without feeling fatigued. You will probably have found during a race that your arms feel like dropping off and that is the limiting factor, not your breathing. There are numerous ways in which this can be overcome but probably the most convenient way is with circuit training.

This form of training is no more than a series of consecutive exercises which are done in rapid succession. You can have circuits without any form of apparatus or more sophisticated ones using weights and gym apparatus. Again, if possible, consult an experienced person in this field who can devise a circuit to cover your particular facilities.

Try to train in a group as the element of competition helps enormously. Do not take a rest between exercises or circuits, but run between each exercise for, in order to gain full value, everything must be done as quickly as possible. If somebody is doing the exercise which you want to do next, do not wait for them to finish but rather do another one. Endeavour to work your circuit so that you are not doing exercises which involve the same muscle groups in succession. Do not cheat in the way you do the exercises or in the number of repetitions—you are only cheating yourself. If you have decided to do the circuits against the watch, do not let the quality of the exercises drop just to achieve a faster completion time.

When doing this form of training it is easy to forget the number of repetitions for each exercise and a useful tip is to write them on a piece of paper or cardboard, placed in position where a number of people working at the same time at different exercises will not interfere with each other. In group training it is desirable to have three grades of circuit so that people of varying ability are catered for, i.e. **A**, **B** and **C**; **A** being the hardest one with the highest number of repetitions.

Always become completely familiar with the circuit and make

sure that you are doing each exercise properly. As your degree of efficiency improves, move to a higher circuit until you are doing three As. Remember that if you are using weights they should be heavy enough to make you work hard but not so large that they stop you from doing the exercises very rapidly. At the end of March the weight training session can be dropped completely and the circuits increased to two periods per week with two days rest in between.

As you can see, there is now a progression from weight to circuits and paddling. Water work cannot be done in many cases in the evenings early in the year but use should be made of the weekends, and try to iron out any faults you may have in your paddling technique. Ask an experienced person to watch you, as it is impossible to see how you are paddling yourself unless you are able to have a cine film made. I would recommend you to have a cine loop taken if possible, as it is very difficult at times to visualize your own faults even if told by somebody else. When the lighter evenings arrive, start paddling once or twice a week initially, progressing into paddling most days of the week, and gradually cutting out the type of training used during the winter months.

RACING TRAINING

As you might expect, there are many conflicting ideas on training but the basis of them all is hard work. I feel that if you are prepared to work hard and sincerely believe in the type of work you are doing, then you can achieve results. It is very important to have a working programme which is aimed at bringing you to peak condition for the major events. Prepare a weekly schedule that fits in with the overall plan, otherwise you may go on to the water without any definite ideas and tend to waste time. Record in your log each day exactly what you have done that evening.

Of course we are not all able to train on ideal water conditions or have the same amount of time available for training, or be training for the same distances, so I would certainly not lay down any hard-and-fast rules as to types of training, particularly when what would suit one person would not do for another. Remember, a schedule must be an individual thing: a general plan could be given to a group but it must be then tailored to suit individual needs.

Because of your winter training you are now capable of facing the demands of the coming racing season with confidence.

You should be feeling fit and well and awaiting eagerly the first race of the year.

Ideally your training will be covering six nights a week with one rest day. To fit this in with the racing programme, Friday should be the rest day as most regattas are held on Saturday. Your programme can be broken down into three light sessions and three heavy sessions, i.e. Monday, Wednesday and Sunday, light sessions and Tuesday, Thursday and Saturday heavy sessions. This does not mean that during the light sessions you do not work hard but rather that you vary the intensity of your programme. A light circuit can be included twice a week in your schedule.

25. A K2 drives through the water towards the end of a long distance race at Oxford

At all times use a stopwatch when training, especially on tidal waters where it is difficult to get accurate distances due to variation in water flow. It is then possible to build up a schedule using lengths of time for sprinting rather than actual distances. For instance, a set of five 2-minute sprints at 70 per cent effort, with a recovery period of 1 minute between each sprint, the set being repeated twice with a 5-minute easy paddle between each set. Another alternative is a pyramid of five 1½-minute sprints with 1-minute recovery periods between each sprint, followed by a 5-minute easy paddle, then four 1-minute sprints, three 30-second sprints, two 20-second sprints, the sprints being separated by suitable recovery periods. Or five 1½-minute sprints, four 2-minute sprints, three 2½-minute sprints, two 3-minute sprints, one 4-minute sprint. The latter being particularly beneficial to 1,000 metre paddlers. Many combinations can be worked out in this manner to suit the individual.

The length of recovery between each sprint is, again, a question of individual fitness and one way of gauging this is taking your pulse after a sprint. Having finished your first sprint, paddle gently for one minute and then take your quarter-minute pulse. This should be 30 or less if you are reasonably fit. If over 30, rest for another half-minute and check your quarter-minute pulse again. It is almost certain that your minute pulse is now down to 120. As soon as the minute pulse is down to 120 you are ready to start work again. Eventually you will find that you will reach the 120 mark inside one minute. It is not necessary to take your pulse after every sprint but take it after the first and second burst of the first set and then work out your recovery period accordingly.

Practise starts constantly, and try and arrange a time trial once a week over an accurately measured course. A time trial over the same stretch of water will give an indication of your progress throughout the season and will also provide valuable experience of paddling over the actual distance that will be raced. For some it may mean travelling a distance to find a suitable course but the effort is well worth while.

During the first few weeks of racing training it is advisable not to try and sprint at 100 per cent effort as your muscles are not ready for a maximum load. Concentrate on build-ups, technique and generally becoming familiar with sprinting. Fartlek training is particularly good at this time of the year where the paddler just sprints for as long as he wishes with no controlled recovery period between each burst. If possible, train in a group where the element of competition is heightened and any one paddler can take the initiative by trying to paddle away from the group.

Before an important competition allow for a period of tapering off your training. I would suggest that approximately ten days before the race you start to shorten the length of your sprints and the intensity of your schedule, until four days before the event you are just doing two sets of 30-second or 20-second bursts. On the third day before the event, have an easy paddle and then take two days off. This should allow you to be fully rested and tuned for the event.

Race Preparation

The end to which all your hard work has been aimed is now in sight. You know your own capabilities and are prepared physically and mentally for the race.

On the day of the event the most important thing is not to become flustered by the hustle and bustle. Check on the times of your events, whether there are heats, semi-finals and finals, and plan your day and meals accordingly. Arrive at the venue in plenty of time and make certain that there have been no alterations to the programme. If it is possible to check the course, do so; this is particularly useful in long-distance racing when portaging is involved.

Inspect your boat and paddles thoroughly, making certain that everything is secured properly and in the right position; there is nothing worse than having to retire from a race because the steering has gone wrong, or the footrest has come loose. Also check your start number with the officials and, if possible, collect it so that it can be fixed to the boat in plenty of time. It is always a good idea to carry spare seat toggles, footrest pins, wing nuts, etc., as these sometimes have the habit of disappearing during a race meeting.

Change into racing kit with time to spare and carry out your warming-up preparations. Some people prefer to warm up twenty minutes before their event and then paddle straight to the start. However, many of the top paddlers are now using the following method of warm-up. One hour and ten minutes before their event they get boated and proceed with warming up for fifteen minutes and then do either a flat out 500 metres for a 1,000-metre race, or 250 metres flat out for a 500-metre race, finishing with a gentle paddle back to the starting point so that the warm-up is finished fifty minutes before the start of the event. If you use this method, wrap up warmly in a tracksuit, etc., after finishing and find somewhere to relax until you are called for your race.

Keep within the range of the Starter's call at the time of the start and paddle around gently until you are called up. Once in your starting position, keep relaxed and control your breathing. If you are on a held start you will have no problem keeping the boat on station, but if you are not held just keep it in position with gentle sculling strokes. Do not be caught napping on the start, listen carefully to what the Starter is saying and have your paddle in the correct position for the word 'Go'.

At the finish do not hang about but rather don a warm tracksuit, or get dressed if you have no more races that day.

10,000-Metre Events

A 10,000-metre event is conducted in a different way to 500-metre and 1,000-metre events. Both tactics and wash hanging come into play and it is necessary for a 10,000-metre paddler to be familiar with these.

Tactics depend entirely on who is in the race and knowing the weak and strong points of your opponents. You have to judge when it is a good moment to try and break away from the bunch, or when to overtake. This will come with experience. Your tactics have to be decided *before* the race, if possible, so that you have a definite picture of what you intend to do. At all times your moves must be fair. It is not gamesmanship to lose your opponent on a buoy or any similar obstruction when you think there is nobody watching! However, it is fair to paddle him off by sprinting away at an angle and then returning to your normal course, so causing him to lose your wash.

Wash hanging is permitted up to the last 1,000 metres of a 10,000-metre event and should be practised in training as any paddler will find it a most useful attribute. It is achieved by placing your bow level with the cockpit of another boat so that you are sitting on the bow wave of the other craft. The canoes should be approximately three feet apart. The psychological effect on your opponent is to your advantage but, in fact, he is not slowed down by you sitting on his wash, and he could have the advantage on bends. Over the last 1,000 metres of this event crews should take a buoyed lane and remain in this lane until the end of the race. I say 'should' as in Britain it is rare to have a 10,000-metre race taking place on water where a buoyed course is laid out. However, over the last 1,000 metres boats should be 3 metres apart and not impede another boat in any way, otherwise a disqualification should be brought into force.

LONG-DISTANCE RACING

This branch of competitive canoeing is extremely popular in this country, and is a challenge which has caught many canoeists' imagination. At some events there are over 200 competitors and the numbers are increasing each year. It is controlled by the Long Distance Racing Committee. At one time events were held under a handicap system, the most well known being the C. N. Davies formula; but today canoes are divided into classes depending on their specifications. L.D. racing has taken tremendous strides forward because British manufacturers have specialized in canoes for this form of racing, and again, the advent of fibreglass and such materials has produced boats far more durable than those made of wood and canvas, and moulded veneers. The paddles are the same as for sprint racing but the L.D. rules stipulate that buoyancy is compulsory for national ranking races and that lifejackets should be carried.

I have covered paddling technique in the previous section on sprint racing and the same technique should be used in long-distance racing events as it is the most efficient way of paddling. I have also covered training but would point out that this would vary on distance on the water as it would be useless to train over a 500-metre stretch for a race covering up to fifteen miles. A schedule should be worked out in the same manner, remembering that an L.D. event can be held during the winter months.

The Long Distance Racing National Coach has produced a booklet entitled *Long Distance Racing*, published by the British Canoe Union, which sets out a suggested schedule for training for L.D. races and provides other useful information.

The ability to handle your craft in all conditions is an essential part of this form of racing. Each course varies: one week you can be paddling on the sea, and the next paddling on a winding narrow stream, or shooting rapids; in fact, you can encounter various conditions in a single event. As mentioned in the sprint section, wash hanging and tactics are another part of L.D. racing and if you become adept at these arts it is another step towards winning a race.

Portaging becomes easier with practice, so try portaging in training, paying particular attention to team work if you are paddling a double. Become familiar with getting in and out at different places, carrying your boat in a comfortable position and making sure you do not lose contact with your paddle. Races can be won or lost at a portage as the vital seconds can be wasted through doing it badly. If you can inspect the portages at a course before the race, do so—picking out where you will land and get afloat again and taking note of any particular hazards.

26. Crews on the Waterside Winter Series (a series of four events run in the early months of each year under some of the hardest conditions) making one of the many portages on the Kennet and Avon Canal

As with sprint racing, arrive at the venue in plenty of time and make certain there have been no alterations to start times. Some events are well organized and there are plenty of marshals to make certain that you do not take a wrong turn on the course, but on occasion the organization is not quite so good, so always try to memorize the course and whether you are able to land at a portage on the left- or right-hand side. Also make a note as to whether it is safe to shoot weirs or whether they have to be portaged.

Long-distance racing can be really good fun. Although many paddlers train seriously for this type of racing, it is not quite so intense as sprinting as there is always an element of luck and, to a certain extent, an element of battling with the varying conditions as well as with your opponents.

ESPADA YOUTH K1 PROJECT

This recent scheme to encourage youth kayak racing is well worth mentioning in this chapter as an important step forward to encouraging racing amongst young people in matched boats. All the kayaks are produced in glass fibre and moulds can be hired or purchased from the British Canoe Union so that youth organisations, schools, clubs, etc., can produce racing boats at a reasonable cost. Also, an Espada K1 can be purchased from registered manufacturers involved in this scheme. Designed by Jorgen Samson of Farum, Denmark in the early 1960's, the original Espada design won several Continental national events, and after slight modification the right to produce it in glass fibre as a one-design boat was passed to the B.C.U. in 1970.

The project has been accepted by the British Schools Canoeing Association, and any person wishing to obtain further details should approach either the present Class Director, Mr. D. R. Cook, via the B.C.U., or the British Schools Canoeing Association.

Having read this chapter on sprint racing and long-distance racing you might ask what is achieved by all this hard work. It is a challenge, it is character building, it develops your mental as well as physical abilities, and the long-term effects of disciplined training and having a healthy body will show in later life.

27. Canoeist on the difficult Granite Fall rapid of the Colorado River in the Grand Canyon. Rapids encountered on the Colorado just cannot be compared with anything in Europe. Major rapids had water far bigger than anything British expedition members had ever seen before, while most lengths were around half to three-quarters of a mile of continuous white water. White water from wall to wall on a river forty to eighty yards across—magnificent!

8

Safety in Canoeing

OLIVER COCK

SOME time ago the Metropolitan Police put out a plea that, should any member of the public see anything untoward happening, or a policeman struggling with a malefactor, he should at once do all he could to stop the malefactor and assist the police. One of the societies which attempts to prevent injury through accident let it be known that they were opposed to this plea by the police; they opined that the public should not go to the assistance of a policeman in difficulties. It is good to know that the public shortly afterwards took the opportunity to show they disagreed with the society's recommendations by coming very much to the assistance of the police in the case of an armed man in a stolen car.

But was the society's recommendation to be safe the right one or not? Is there any way to be certainly safe in life? Is it not better to meet the danger, to be prepared for it and to know what to do when it happens, *before it happens*?

This chapter heading may have the same effect on some readers as the police plea did on the society—'If canoeing is dangerous—better not canoe'. But this attitude is a negative one. If it is carried into life it produces no progress, and no progress is progress backwards when viewed by those who are going forwards. The second attitude is surely the better one: if there are dangers ahead, let us find out what these dangers are; let us learn how to deal with them; and then, when they appear, we shall know what to do, and the situation will come quickly under control.

Dr. Sol Rosenthal, Professor of Preventative Medicine at the University of Illinois, has pointed out that to take part in a risky exercise produces a state of well-being in the participant which can border on euphoria. Even more important, this euphoria is lasting and constructive, as opposed to the unhappy drug addict whose state of euphoria is not lasting and is destructive. The reasons for this are very complicated and need not be gone into here, but the fact certainly remains worth noting.

All adventurous activities necessarily have a modicum of danger about them, otherwise they would not be adventurous. Come to that, some of the less adventurous activities contain an element of risk—even at cricket one may be hit and injured by a flying ball. When one comes to deal with activities which involve the elements, or physical features of the countryside, these risks are greatly increased. Thus in gliding, immense care is taken to ensure that the glider is in perfect condition; in rock climbing, every precaution is taken against falls. What should one do when one comes upon an activity dealing with water?

Whichever of the elements one is dealing with, the important thing is to learn something about it. You cannot glide without knowing which way the wind is blowing. You do not wisely climb on crumbling rock. Equally, with any given piece of water, you should discover what is likely to happen when you get involved with it.

There are a number of ways one can enjoy oneself on the water, but, whatever one is going to do, the First Law of Safety is:

LEARN TO SWIM

And by swimming is not meant just a pleasant bathe in a warm swimming pool, with people around to pull you out if necessary, but in an ice-cold river, or in a lake, or at sea with the waves buffeting you. Can you swim there? Are you happy there? If you are, you are likely to be safe.

But why all this fuss about swimming? *You* are going canoeing. *You* have no intention of going swimming! We agree; but every enthusiastic canoeist has found himself swimming at some time or other. It is the unexpectedness of it which makes it dangerous. If you are ready for the swim, then there is nothing dangerous in it. Therefore the next item on the agenda to make you safe is practising swimming from your canoe. What is it like suddenly to be flung into the water? What is it like if your canoe fills with water and founders? What is it like suddenly to be turned upside down under it? Can you get out? How do you get out? Well, better to choose a time and a place where it is reasonably comfortable, and where you can organize some friends to come to your help if necessary. If you don't like it the first time, do it again and again until you begin to enjoy it—and, we promise you, in time you will. And when you enjoy it, you will be safe.

Perhaps we had better look at this capsizing game more closely, because there are rules which will ensure your always being able to get out of your canoe if you obey them. Here is how to do it, then, when you are learning in your comfortable surroundings, with your friends around to help if necessary.

CAPSIZE DRILL

First of all, make quite certain that you are alone in your cockpit—that is, that you are not sharing it with loose ends of rope, or bags of equipment, or *anything else whatever*. There is no surer way of getting jammed in your canoe when you capsize than by being slack about this point.

Now proceed as follows:

1. Put your paddle beside you, floating on the water.

2. Lean forward and grasp the gunwales as far forward as you can reach. You are now looking into the cockpit or at the deck of your canoe. You must remain looking that way until you are entirely clear of the canoe, underneath it.

3. Capsize.

4. Remain looking into the cockpit or at the deck, release your grasp of the gunwales.

5. If you have a spray cover on, release this, either from the cockpit coaming, or from yourself if it is the type that is fixed to the canoe.

6. Still looking into the cockpit or at the deck, put your hands beside your hips, on the side of your canoe, and push yourself out. Be sure not to kick with your legs—let them slide smoothly out of the cockpit. Aim to go downwards as you leave the canoe—this will ensure the clean exit of your body and legs. Too hasty an attempt to break the surface may mean that you will get stuck in the cockpit. It will also allow air to escape from the upturned canoe.

7. When you are clear of the canoe, swim to the surface, collect your paddle if you can, swim to one end of the canoe and hold it. Don't otherwise interfere with it. Neither try to right it, nor roll it over, nor climb on to it. By all these means you will waterlog your canoe and lose a life raft.

8. Swim to the side, towing or pushing your canoe, swimming how you like.

9. At the side empty it, or get your friends to help you empty it, and carry on.

With practice, this drill will become a habit, and when you capsize accidentally you will easily be able to cope with the situation. You will be safe.

PREPARING FOR THE UNEXPECTED

Now let us look at the Second Law of Safety. This is a very common law of life, well known yet seldom recognized until it is too late. It is the law which allows the unexpected always to happen. Usually known as the Eternal Law of Cussedness, it is also sometimes called Fingle's Law. There seems no reason for this, but that is the way of the Eternal Law of Cussedness, and Mr Fingle—whoever he may have been—is a very good friend, to be kept up your sleeve.

The truth is that canoeing is enormous fun. If you are continually expecting the unexpected to happen, then it isn't unexpected, is it? If you are prepared for the unexpected to happen, then, when it does happen you are not frightened by it and all is well. The dangerous factor—the killing factor—in all this is being unprepared, and consequently panicking. When a person panics, all collected, coherent thought leaves him. He is useless, powerless, and a menace to any who come to his help.

If Fingle's Law dogs one through life anyway, it certainly dogs a canoeist's life. Because the permutations and combinations of unexpectedness are infinite, it would take more than a lifetime for one to be fully prepared for all eventualities. A list of all the things that might happen would be infinite, too; but experience has shown that some things occur more often than others. We have already dealt with two of them, swimming and capsizing. Let us make a short list of the other things one should or should not do (Fig. 40).

In our list of 'do's and don't's', why are these chosen as most important to canoeists? We have already dealt with some, so we will not mention these again.

Buoyancy
Buoyancy prevents you and your canoe from sinking. Buoyancy for the canoe is easy, so long as you use common sense. It means

DO's and DON'T's for CANOEISTS !!!

DON'T canoe if you cannot swim

DO provide buoyancy: always air bags in your boat, and a life-jacket for yourself where a capsize would be dangerous—in the sea, heavy rapids, floods, and cold water.

DO ask about local conditions: tides, currents, rapids, and weather changes can all be dangerous.

DON'T go out alone without having told someone where you are going and how long you think you will be.

DON'T put more people in a canoe than it is designed to carry.

DON'T wear wellingtons. You cannot swim in heavy boots.

DON'T change places

DO keep clear of of other craft.

DO keep away from weirs. They are dangerous.

DON'T right a capsized canoe. Hang on to it. It will float and you may not.

DON'T be put off by this list. It is all common sense really.

DO REMEMBER —better safe than sorry.

DO learn to canoe properly, and take the B.C.U. Tests

Fig. 40

bags of air held in the canoe, so that when the canoe fills with water it doesn't sink. Anything that holds air and does not leak will do. Even your clothes packed into a waterproof bag hold enough air to keep the canoe afloat. Distribute the air bags in the canoe and make them secure so that, even when it is full of water, it will float on an even keel. We have seen a man who had put buoyancy into one end of his canoe only, trying to rescue something which looked like Cleopatra's Needle as it floated off downstream. We have also seen a canoe sink to the bottom of the river with two airbags left floating wistfully on the surface to mark the point of its descent!

The Lifejacket
Personal buoyancy is a much more complex affair, and a very great deal has been written and discovered recently about life-saving equipment. It all started when the Consumers' Association and the British Standards Institution discovered themselves both investigating the position in 1962. The Consumer's Association issued a report through their journal *Which?* showing that there were very few life-*saving* jackets at all, but a great many jackets on the market purporting to be life-saving jackets which in fact bordered on being murderous.

After much experimentation, and assistance from the Royal Navy and others, some of the features of a life-saving jacket are now becoming known and understood. There is much more to learn, but the British Standards Institution has published a standard with which all lifejackets should comply.

Besides quality of material, which is of course vital, but which need not bother you as a purchaser, provided the jacket has the BSI kite-mark on it, what are the important features of a life-jacket?

(*a*) The lifejacket must be satisfactory under the worst possible conditions, that is to say, supporting an unconscious person in rough water.

(*b*) It must under no circumstances slip off over the head.

(*c*) Vital nerves leave the head via the back and side of the neck, and these must be kept as warm as possible. Therefore the jacket must fit even more snugly round the neck.

(*d*) In order that the patient's face be kept as far out of the water as possible, the buoyancy of the jacket must support him round the neck, tilting him backwards at an angle of approximately 45 degrees, leaving his legs to dangle as they will.

(e) *At least* 35 pounds of buoyancy are required to accelerate a body which has just slid down one wave to going up the next. Less buoyancy will mean that his head may go *through* the next wave instead of *over* it.

(f) Since the patient is slung on his back at an angle of 45 degrees, there will be a larger proportion of buoyancy in front of than behind him. This means that, should he have his back to the oncoming waves, his head will pass through them before the buoyancy has had a chance to lift him up over them. Therefore the jacket must contrive to turn him round quickly, to face into the oncoming waves. Due to the velocities of water within a wave, which cause the water to rise and fall as the wave progresses, 45 degrees was found also to be the correct angle at which the patient should be held in the water, to induce his automatically facing the waves.

The BSI also ruled that the jacket should put the patient into the right position in the water in a maximum of three seconds, without any effort on his part; that it should be easy to put on in half a minute; that it should be equipped with a plastic whistle, so that he could draw attention to himself without taking the skin off his lips; and that it should be fitted with a lifting becket, so that rescuers could get him easily out of the water.

So much, then, for the general characteristics of a life-saving jacket; but there are some which are peculiar to canoeists. Canoeing is a hot recreation, so the jacket must be sufficiently ventilated to allow the sweat to evaporate. There must be no chafing of the arm or neck of the wearer. A capsize always occurs unexpectedly; therefore the jacket must be worn at all times; therefore it must be comfortable. In a capsize, buoyancy of as much as 35 pounds may push the canoeist up into his canoe and prevent him escaping from it; but he must have some buoyancy in his jacket to ensure his coming to the surface. A figure of approximately $13\frac{1}{2}$ pounds has been found satisfactory for this. Nevertheless he must be able easily to increase this buoyancy to the requisite 35 pounds whilst he is swimming, should he be in the water for any length of time.

These are not easy conditions to fulfil, but there are life-saving jackets which comply with these requirements, having an inherent buoyancy of $13\frac{1}{2}$ pounds which can be increased easily to 35 pounds either by oral inflation or by manually operated bottle, though the latter adds very considerably to the cost. Automatic inflation cannot be accepted, as this has to operate within three seconds, and this does not necessarily allow the canoeist time to escape from his upturned craft.

Life-saving jackets having the BSI kite-mark cannot be cheap, but what are *you* worth? There are things on the market sold as lifejackets, which will drown you as easily as anything will. They cost 50 pence or so. Is this a wise economy?

Overloading
A canoe becomes grossly unstable if it is overloaded. A canoe designed to carry one person will be unsafe with two people in it. Besides, very often the cockpit is not big enough to allow two people in together. They have to get in one at a time, and get out the same way. That is all very well the right way up, but what about upside down?

Footwear
If you cannot swim in heavy boots, you certainly cannot swim in wellingtons. Besides which, the loose top rim of the wellington allows you to get into the canoe all right, but catches in the framework when you try to get out—especially when upside down and in a hurry. Do not, however, canoe in bare feet. Our rivers all too often contain broken bottles, tins, and other sharp objects—cut feet are always unpleasant and often go septic. Avoid them by wearing gym shoes.

Changing places
Have you ever tried changing places on a tandem bicycle without getting off first? A canoe is also a very tippy vehicle. If you want to change places, get to the bank or beach, and do it there.

Collisions
A canoe is not only tippy, it is light and frail. If you take on any other vessel, you are going to be the loser. Therefore just get out of the way. Remember, too, that you may well not be visible to a larger craft. If you are ever run down by a power-driven boat, you will be very lucky if you escape very severe injury from the propellor blades.

Weirs
Take it that weirs are dangerous. You will see photographs and films of experts shooting them, and playing about below them, but they are experts. They know what they are doing, and they have learnt to interpret the movements of the water until they

can judge what is safe and what is dangerous. Very often a weir that looks safe to shoot is more dangerous than one that looks dangerous. Only tackle a weir when accompanied by an experienced canoeist.

Distress Flares
This is another item which it is essential to have with you if you are going into open waters such as the sea, estuaries or large lakes. Here again the Consumers' Association has issued a report, and again the peculiar requirements of the canoeist must be borne in mind before rushing out to buy.

The flare is going to be operated at water level, most probably *in* the water. Therefore it must be waterproof, even to the extent of operating under the water for a few seconds. To be carried conveniently in a canoe it must be small. Smoke disperses too quickly in a high wind and may be missed. The best flare therefore is a bright red one, lasting a minute if possible. Quite small and economic flares which do all this are available from ships' chandlers, and every sea canoeist should have some. They are called Red Hand Flares.

Crash Helmets
Occasionally you will see canoeists shooting rapids, wearing crash helmets. The canoeists are usually experts and the rapids dangerous. Their precaution is a wise one since a capsize might result in the canoeist hitting his head on a rock and knocking himself out. Special helmets are made for canoeists which allow the water to drain out immediately. These are rather specialized pieces of equipment and do not usually concern the ordinary canoeist.

KEEP YOUR EQUIPMENT IN GOOD ORDER

We have so far been dealing with equipment which is special to emergencies. But it is equally important that all equipment should be in good working order. We are reminded of the incident of the small boy who was heard to exclaim: 'Sir! Sir! This canoe doesn't function!' Whereupon he rolled slowly over, to reveal a hole through which 'Sir' could easily have pushed both fists together. It is only common sense that the hull itself be kept in functioning order before, during and after one goes afloat. A proper repair kit appropriate to your canoe must be carried.

Paddles

These must be well maintained. If a paddle breaks during a trip the canoeist is helpless; therefore many prudent canoeists carry a second paddle with them for just this emergency. If it is of a jointed variety, the joint should not be sloppy. If this does happen, soaking in water for some hours will usually swell the wood again and tighten it.

Spray Covers

These have become an important piece of equipment. Most modern ones are designed to stay with the canoeist, rather than remain on the canoe. If yours is one of these, then it must be secure round the waist, otherwise it may slip down and hinder your swimming. Such spray covers must also easily come off the cockpit coaming, and a round cockpit is more likely to ensure this than an angular one. Besides, it is not easy to make corners really waterproof, and a leak, even on the deck, may lead you into trouble if the water is rough enough. Spray covers of this type should have some sort of release strap by which you can pull them away from the coaming quickly and easily should they be reluctant to come away by themselves.

If the cover is designed to stay with the canoe, then it must stay there. It should not be able to break loose, even half way. And you must be able to escape clean away from it. A zip fastener looks very tidy, and usually zips satisfactorily. The time when it won't is when you are upside down and Fingle has got hold of it. Then how do you get out?

Painters

These cause more argument among canoeists than any other item of equipment. Obviously they must be sound, to prevent them letting you down. There must be provision for one at both ends of the canoe, otherwise you will find yourself always wanting it at the end where you have not got it. However it is arranged, it should never have the chance to become loose while you are afloat, otherwise, somehow, it will tangle on you at the very moment you want to be free. There is even argument for doing it up into a hank and pushing it into the kangaroo pouch of your anorak, safely out of the way but immediately available when you want it.

Glass-fibre canoes, with their very slippery hulls, must have at least a loop of line at the bow and stern, in order to give people something to hold them by. The line must be at least 6 millimetres in diameter, and the loop big enough to insert all your fingers through, otherwise you stand to have your fingers cut off if the canoe decides to roll over. In fact, it is better to fit a very short line and toggle at these points, and the toggle ought to be four inches long for you to be able to hold on to it properly.

TAKE LESSONS

It is no good your having perfect equipment if you don't know how to use it. Just as with a bicycle it is useless if you cannot balance it, so with a canoe you must have a sound basic technique. A few people pick this up naturally, without being taught or shown; but the easier way is to have lessons, when it will not be necessary to discover everything by trial and error. There are only a few basic skills in canoeing. When you have learnt these, and practised them until you can use them at the appropriate moment without wasting time thinking what you ought to do next, you will be well on your way to becoming a proficient and safe canoeist.

RESCUE METHODS

On the River

Having, as we hope, persuaded you that old Fingle is going to get hold of you at some time or other, however hard you try to avoid him, let us now turn to methods by which you may get yourself out of predicaments, and how you may also assist others out of theirs.

First, here are some suggestions about tours on rivers.

Like any other expedition, river trips must be properly prepared for. Not only must local knowledge be obtained, particularly with regard to the weather, fallen trees and other obstructions, but the BCU *Guide to Waterways* should be consulted if the expedition is in this country; if abroad, then consult the relevant national canoe association—their addresses are given at the end of this book.

The minimum size of *any* canoeing party should be three. The ideal maximum size of a party is between six and eight. Any party which is larger should always be split into smaller groups. Before going on the river, everyone must know who is in charge, who is to go down first, and, most important of all, who is the last man. The leader of the expedition will not necessarily go first. In fact he is more likely to choose a reliable aide-de-camp and send him on ahead, whilst he remains right at the back, acting as 'Tail-End Charlie' to make sure that everyone in the party is safe. A whistle is extremely useful, and simple signals should be agreed upon.

The party should never become separated. Frequent pauses must be made—the leader will wait for 'Tail-end Charlie', whose arrival will guarantee that the party is complete.

In his chapter on slalom and white water canoeing, Ken Langford gives some more advanced advice on the behaviour of rough water. For the average canoeist on the average British river, the following remarks will be helpful and probably sufficiently comprehensive:

In general, paddle firmly, above all when approaching and going through faster water. By doing this, you keep steerage way on your canoe and thus control over it. If you are swung broadside and right round by the current just before a rapid, it is far better to continue down backwards rather than run the risk of being caught in the broadside position, when you will inevitably hit an obstruction, almost certainly capsize and probably damage your canoe.

The water will always flow fastest through its deepest part, and for this reason always canoe round the outside bend of a river. Aim your canoe at the fastest water in a rapid—the force of the water itself will keep you clear of most rocks.

OBSTACLES

There is an important difference between natural obstacles lying in the river—mainly rocks, large boulders, etc.—and obstacles hanging over the water or put there by man—overhanging trees, posts with barbed wire, general garbage, etc. Keep clear of overhanging trees and other comparable obstacles which have no effect on the flow of the current, otherwise you will find yourself pinned against them and in a potentially dangerous situation. Tree trunks which have been uprooted and carried off downstream, and then wedged across a rapid, are particularly dangerous. This is another reason for always reconnoitring a rapid from the bank, however well you think you know it from previous trips.

The first confusion that most often arises is the sudden stopping of the canoe as it floats over an apparently unobstructed and smooth piece of water. You have found an underwater obstruction, which we hope will not be so sharp as to tear a hole in the bottom of your canoe. The most likely method of freeing the canoe is to retire again, by exactly the same route by which you had arrived. If this is impossible you may have to get out; but before you do this, feel down on both sides of the canoe, with your paddle or your hand, or look down, to see if the obstruction sticks out on one side or the other. If it does, step out on that side, as it cannot be more than a few inches deep, and you will only get your feet wet. Step out on the other side, and you may well disappear under water. This will amuse your friends, if not you. If the obstruction has holed your canoe, you are going to get wet anyway, so the quicker you get out the better. Then the canoe will rise quickly and you may be able to get it ashore before it gets too water-logged.

Sometimes, when the river is flowing fast, the canoe will be slewed round sideways against the rock it has hit, and the whole pressure of the current will press it against the rock. On no account allow the canoe to tip over upstream, so that the water can flow into the cockpit. Press hard on the downstream gun-wale and get out as quickly as you can. If you get out on the downstream side of the canoe, be careful that the sudden lightening of it does not free it and let it knock you off your feet. If you get out on the upstream side you may get wetter, but it may be safer.

If the canoe does fill with water, it may be necessary to tear a hole in the downstream side of one end, so that the water pressure can be released and that end dragged round, upstream, to allow the canoe to slide off its obstruction.

Whatever happens, remember your capsize drill, and try to remain with your canoe. If by mischance you lose your paddle, your friends who are with you—for you should never paddle alone—can be despatched to gather it up. The only time when you should abandon your canoe is when you are being borne down upon some major danger, such as a weir or a waterfall. Then leave your canoe and swim as fast as you can to the side.

TAKE THE SHORTEST WAY

And talking of swimming to the side, swimmers are very slow. In clothes they are slower still. In clothes and towing a canoe they are even slower. It is imperative to get to the side as quickly as possible, even if it is only to be able to get into your canoe again and go on. Since you are so slow in the water, you must go by the shortest possible route. The shortest distance between a point (you) and a line (the bank) is at right angles to the line. Therefore swim directly towards the bank, even though you are being carried downstream by the current. You may end up some hundred yards down the river; but you will have got to the bank by the quickest possible route.

Just before or in rapids keep firm hold of one end of your canoe and follow it through the rapids. It will of its own accord find the deepest water and the safest passage, and will also protect you from the rocks.

EMPTYING YOUR CANOE

At the bank if your canoe is light, it may be possible for you to empty it by yourself without the assistance of your friends. Being at one end of your canoe, first establish a firm foothold. Now lift your end of the canoe as high as you can. When the water has finished pouring out, turn it over, up in the air. Then put it down, push your end down and hold it there until all the water remaining in the canoe has run to your end. Then, putting one hand underneath, and the other on top, lift the canoe up and turn it over in one gesture. Continue to do this until all the water has come out of the canoe.

If the canoe is too heavy to do this, or there is too much water in it, two people are needed to empty it, one at each end. Throughout the initial operation the canoe must be kept on a dead even keel, fore and aft. Both people start lifting it slightly, and roll it over sideways until one edge of the cockpit coaming comes above the surface of the water. This breaks the airlock and the canoe will immediately start to rise. No one must hurry and the canoe must be kept level. As it comes up, the canoe will be rolled properly upside down again. When it is clear of the water, each person should lift his end in turn, until the canoe is again empty.

Some types of canoe have coamings specially contrived not to allow all the water out. The only thing to do with these canoes is to operate with two people, as above. Then, when all the water possible has been released by ordinary means, the canoe should be returned to a level, upside-down position above the water, and shaken by rolling from side to side until again all the water possible has been emptied out. After that there should only be a very little water left inside which, if you are fussy, you will have to mop up with a sponge.

Sometimes it is possible to lodge the far end of the canoe on the bank or on a rock. You then proceed as though with two people until the canoe is virtually empty. Then revert to the push-down/lift-up method, as with one person.

SMALL RAPIDS

The noise of falling water and the drop of the river in front of you will announce the rapid. You ought to know, from previous study of the map and the appropriate river guide, whether it is a severe one or not. If an easy one, the first man will go through some 30 yards ahead, thus allowing the second man time to avoid a collision and find a new route if the first man hits an obstruction. The rest of the party follow at similar intervals.

MORE SEVERE RAPIDS

Reconnaissance from the bank is essential. Careful note must be made beforehand of a nearby landmark so that the party can pull in to the bank in good time. Allow the most experienced canoeist to go through first, observed from the bank by the remainder. Only one canoeist should take the rapids at a time. The whole party must wait in the first pool of quiet water until the last man is through and the party is complete again. No shame whatsoever is attached to portaging around a fall which is too severe for one's degree of experience.

At Sea

Much useful information about safety at sea is included in Chris Hare's chapter on coastal touring. The repetition here of some of the main points will emphasize their importance.

1. Wear a BSI kite-marked life-jacket (best of all, the BCU approved life-jacket as advertised in canoeing magazines). So-called buoyancy aids are not adequate.

2. Pay particular attention to the state of your equipment. Salt water is harmful to all kinds of material, and sand inside a canvas canoe can wreak havoc between the ribs and the canoe skin. The efficiency of your buoyancy may be a life-saving matter.

3. Wear bright clothing. Orange is best, and excellent orange anoraks are available. Your canoe too should be a bright colour, easily visible at a long distance.

4. Three is the absolute minimum size of a party. Solo canoeing at sea is madness.

5. Take whistles and have a simple set of whistle and hand signals.

6. Consult knowledgeable local people—fishermen and harbour masters are best—about the local conditions.

7. Obtain the latest weather report from the nearest meteorological office.

8. Inform a reliable friend or a member of the family about your time and place of departure, your route, and your estimated time and place of arrival. Inform them when you land.

9. Adopt a definite formation at sea, with one nominated person in front and another to bring up the rear, no canoe being more than one minute's paddling time away from another, and all canoeists well positioned to keep an eye on one another all the time. The leader should be free to move around the party and keep in touch with everyone.

10. Experienced canoeists spurn the presence of a powered rescue boat, and their independence is for them one of the attractions of sea canoeing. But the less experienced should be under no illusions about the dangers of the sea. The rescue drills which follow must be known—and known well—by everyone who ventures out; or the party must be accompanied by a power boat manned by a competent seaman with good local knowledge. Longer trips away from the coast should not be undertaken, even when accompanied by a rescue boat, without considerable training in overcoming the danger and discomfort of cramp and general fatigue when confined in a small canoe cockpit.

11. Learn and practise the Deep Water Rescue as often as possible. Capsizes tend to occur very quickly one after the other at sea, and the only sure preventative against panic is a high standard of training.

12. Do not hesitate to 'raft up' frequently to prevent fatigue setting in; but remember that a group of canoes rafted together will drift very quickly with current and wind.

13. In fact, always try not to work against current and wind.

14. Learn the Eskimo Roll!

One of the joys of being advanced in anything is that one knows the rules of the game, and also when they must be broken. We mentioned earlier that in the capsize drill you must always leave your canoe upside down. In very heavy waves, however, as at sea, there is an argument for righting the canoe as quickly as possible; but we hope you will never find yourself in such conditions, until you too are an advanced canoeist. In a heavy sea, if the canoe is left upside down, the airlock at the cockpit will be broken as the waves pass, and the canoe will fill up fairly quickly, and become waterlogged. The method of righting it under these conditions is then carried out like this. Having blown up his life-jacket to maximum buoyancy, the canoeist goes to one side of his canoe, amidships, only holding it enough to prevent it from moving away. At that position he pushes his side upwards, with maximum thrust, trying as it were to chuck the canoe into the air. This will roll the canoe over to the right way up, with the minimum possible amount of water in it. This drill should be done as quickly as possible after the capsize, after which the canoeist returns once more to one end, where he holds on again, awaiting his friends' assistance.

The recognized method of putting someone back into his canoe again at sea is known as the

Deep Water Rescue Drill

This rescue is used when the 'patient' has done the capsize drill and is out of his canoe. Here is one rescue drill. Usually, at least two rescuers are needed.

The two canoes come up to the capsized one, to form a letter H. Both rescuers should face the same way, towards the on-coming waves. The patient should swim round to the outside of one of the rescuing canoes, and hold the cockpit coaming there. If there is another canoeist available, he should go to the outside of the other canoe and do likewise (Plates 28 and 29).

Both rescuers then proceed to lift the canoe, on a dead even keel, emptying it as for two people on the river's edge. As the casualty rises, it should be drawn across the decks of the two rescue boats to form a very stable catamaran. If there are only the two rescuers, then the one with the swimmer will start his lift slightly behind the other, so as to take a slightly greater load, since he cannot tip inwards because of the weight of the swimmer on his outside. It may be advisable for each rescuer to put his inward hand on top of the casualty, and do the lifting with his outward hand. This position of the hands is that of one of the rolls, and it will help him to right himself should he begin to capsize inwards.

28 & 29.   The deep-water rescue

Having emptied and righted the canoe, the two rescuers put it down between them, draw themselves together on it, and make a raft by holding their paddles across them. The bow of the patient's canoe should now face aft of the rescuers' canoes, and the patient should go to *their* bows (Plate 30). He will now be just behind his own cockpit, between his own canoe and that of one of the rescuers. The other rescuer slides back along the empty canoe so that he can lean heavily on its fore deck. The patient can now press upon the decks of the canoes on either side of him and throw his feet into his own cockpit, immediately sliding into his seat, when he is soon ready to set off again.

With practice this rescue can be done under pretty severe conditions, excluding only actual breaking surf. Coolness and competence are more important than speed (except perhaps occasionally on a river, e.g. above a weir). Unlike the Eskimo Rescue which follows, it can be done equally well with doubles as with singles.

THE ESKIMO RESCUE

When an Eskimo capsizes at sea and is unable to right his canoe again, perhaps because he has lost his paddle, he has very quickly to be rescued by a fellow hunter, yet without getting out of his canoe, for trying to swim in those icy waters would be fatal. We have adopted their technique of rescue. Incidentally, it helps greatly to build up your confidence under water. It can only be done with a canoe which has a tight-fitting spray cover, and which fits you tightly, and with a suitable knee-grip. It is no good if you fall out of the canoe as

30. The deep-water rescue

31. The two-man Eskimo rescue:
    bow grip method

soon as you turn upside down. Practise as follows: position your own canoe at right angles to a friend's canoe. Grasp his bow firmly. Lean over until your shoulder is in the water and pull yourself upright (Plate 31). Repeat this exercise, leaning further over each time until you are eventually hanging completely upside down. Next, send your friend a few feet away, turn upside down, and wait for him to guide his bow into your hands. Repeat, sending him further and further away each time. Now, when you capsize, bang the sides of your boat firmly to attract his attention, then wave your hands back and forth on either side and above your boat to make it easier for you to find his bow. This is particularly important if the water is dirty and you cannot see anything. As you gain confidence, you will find that you can swim up on one side for a breath of air whilst waiting for your rescuer. This is the best possible training against panicking in an upturned canoe that we know.

A useful variation of the Eskimo Rescue is for the rescuer to bring his boat parallel to the capsized canoe. The rescuer places his paddle at right angles over his own cockpit and the bottom of the upturned canoe. He guides the hands of the canoeist under the water on to the shaft of the paddle between the two boats (Plate 32). The canoeist in trouble then pulls himself up. This variation is particularly valuable in rough water at sea: there is much less danger of the rescuer's bows driving through the side of the other canoe; and the canoeist who has been rescued is at once in a very stable position, firmly linked as he is with his rescuer's canoe.

32. The two-man Eskimo rescue: paddle grip method

THE ESKIMO ROLL

This is the technique which makes a canoeist really safe under all conditions. It is now a requirement of the Advanced Sea Proficiency Test. Don't try to learn it on your own, but join a club where you can receive expert instruction. Many people achieve their first roll after only twenty minutes' instruction, although it takes many more hours' training and experience to become really proficient.

There is, however, no known guaranteed method for a single man to get himself back into his canoe alone, after he has come out. Therefore let us finish with a final law:

Never canoe alone.

9

Canoe Design

JORGEN SAMSON

PADDLING is the oldest method of boat propulsion. The prehistoric man undoubtedly used a piece of a branch as a paddle, riding astride a tree-trunk. A few thousands of years later his palaeolithic descendant made the first improvement in canoe design, the dug-out, hollowed by means of fire and pointed at the ends by means of a stone axe.

In Europe, dug-outs were used everywhere and in Sweden the last 'ege' disappeared only 150 years ago. In Hungary real canoes, also kayaks, were used for exercise as early as 1625. The name comes from the Spanish *canoa* (parallels: French *canot* and German *Kahn*) and refers to a great many types, all being narrow, and pointed in their ends. They are propelled with a paddle single or double bladed without any support on the boat so that the man is facing forward.

The appearance of canoes has always been impressive. The famous Swedish artist, Albert Engström, was a great admirer of their shape. He kept two kayaks hanging under the ceiling in his atelier. 'One can sit for hours admiring the beauty in the lines,' he said.

Canoes, however, are not made exclusively for the eye; they are given their shape to fulfil the demands of performance which may differ considerably.

If a canoe builder tells you that his canoe is perfect for every purpose, then do not trust him. The true all-round canoe should be narrow and beamy, high and low built, flat and rockered and that is why he did not build it. On the other hand, his canoe could be just the boat you need, possessing most of the qualities which are essential to your particular purpose.

The shape and the material in a canoe is decided by its use; racing or touring, open or sheltered water, rapid rivers or calm lakes. Furthermore, canoeists are typical individualists, each with his personal taste and special demands. The writer

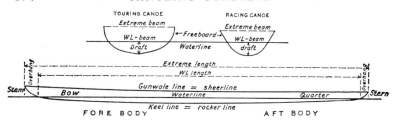

Fig. 41 Terms in canoe design

of this chapter also has his own ideas and prefers to express them definitely rather than trying to find the average meaning of the subject: the relationship between canoe form and performance.

Some abbreviations will probably be useful:

L—Length (maximum)
B—Beam (maximum)
LWL—Length on the waterline
BWL—Beam on the WL
WL—Waterline of the loaded canoe
DL—Draught, loaded
D—Displacement = Total weight of canoe, man and paddle
PC—Prismatic coefficient = fineness of the canoe; can be expressed as a value derived from the formula:

$$\frac{D \text{ (in cubic feet)}}{\text{Area of the widest section (in square feet)} \times L \text{ (in feet)}}, \text{ where}$$

a value of more than 0·55 indicates a full form and one below indicates a fine form in the sense that the canoe is narrow in its bow and quarter.

We will also have to use terms such as 'sheerline' and 'rocker' which mean the curvature of the gunwale and the keel (Fig. 41).

The performance of any canoe can be discussed only if we define the different qualities concerned.

STABILITY

Stability is the resistance against rolling and depends upon the location of the centre of gravity and the centre of buoyancy. If a boat is leaned so much that the former falls outside the latter, it will capsize (Fig. 42). Fortunately, this inconvenient behaviour can be counteracted in various ways:

Fig. 42 Stability

1. Keep the centre of gravity low—simply by sitting low.
2. Choose a canoe in which the centre of buoyancy moves much when it is leaned. In other words, choose a beamy canoe in which the submerged side is buoyant enough to resist the rolling.
3. Move the centre of gravity with your body opposite the leaning.

In a C1 (racing Canadian canoe) the lack of stability is evident, it would roll over if the paddler was stiff like a doll. He is not, however, and his ability to balance his body makes up for the lack of natural stability of the canoe. This example is the most extreme we have, but we face what is special to canoeing. The canoe itself cannot fully support its paddler when leaned, for instance, in waves. To achieve full support we need a beam of at least 40 inches and the canoe has changed to a dinghy.

In a tippy racing canoe the sector of stability is very small so that quick reactions are essential. In the beamy touring canoe there is more time to react, but in both cases the canoeist moves his body instinctively.

It is seen that beam makes for stability and, of course, it also gives buoyancy. The resulting shape might be an 'airship', easy for wind and waves to handle, but difficult and tiresome for the canoeist. This factor, however, belongs to the seaworthiness and we will return to it later.

Within a certain beam the shape of the sections can vary greatly and the difference in stability is considerable.

The U—or Box-Shape cross section gives most stability as the centre of buoyancy moves much when leaning the canoe. If the U-shape is used in narrow kayaks under 53 cm. beam they feel safe because of a good initial stability, but their final stability is relatively small.

The V-Shape cross section can either be flat in its angle and possess a stability only little inferior to the U-form or it can be steeper and unstable. The canoe is then felt to be top heavy and it is inclined to lie over on either side, obviously hating the upright position.

The Round Shape cross section gives stability only if the ratio $\frac{BWL}{DL}$ is great enough, i.e. when the part of the section below WL makes a flat arch. Decreasing $\frac{BWL}{DL}$ to the value 2·0 means a true semi-circular cross section below WL, at which point any stability is lost. Regardless of the form, this ratio should never fall below 5·0 in touring canoes and 3·1 in racers.

Combinations of the above mentioned forms are common. In touring canoes the U-shape is given a flat V underneath (Fig. 41). The result is more final than initial stability and a limitation of buoyancy. All modern racing canoes are V-shaped above the WL and round below and the stability, particularly the final part, is very poor.

The rocker will also influence stability. A small amount of rocker will decrease stability because of the small $\frac{BWL}{DL}$ ratio in bow and quarter. A large amount of rocker has the opposite effect and will also lower the centre of gravity a little.

SEAWORTHINESS

Seaworthiness is the ability to maintain stability, speed and course in a seaway. A canoe which is stable in calm water is not unconditionally safe in the sea. If it were so, we should expect to find the maximum of safety in a beamy Canadian touring canoe. This type, however, while highly regarded on inland water, is not considered safe enough on the open sea.

The Canadian has much buoyancy and little draught. This makes it skid or yaw in solid following waves and in spite of its stability it cannot be considered a safe sea boat.

The touring kayaks are the superior craft for open sea canoeing, but the most beamy of them are difficult to handle in a strong wind and waves.

The U-shape, if beamy and flat, is so stable that it will follow the profile of any wave coming from the side. This is felt in a

Fig. 43 The U-shape in a strong wind and waves

hard rolling tendency and if a wave is breaking just on your side, you will have a big job to do. First, by leaning your body very hard against the breaker in order to sustain the heel which tends to be as steep as the wave; next, when the wave has passed you must immediately change your weight over to the opposite side in order not to fall out of the canoe. In fact, it is easier to control a boat which is not quite as stable (Fig. 43).

The V-shape reduces the buoyancy and the initial stability and it also contributes to good directional stability. The latter is important, especially when the waves are coming on the quarter. Waves from this direction cause much more trouble than a true following sea as the canoe is constantly 'broaching to', i.e., turning parallel to the waves (Fig. 44). In these circumstances, a flat bottom with excessive rocker can be dangerous even if the canoe is felt to be stable enough.

A small amount of rocker is advisable and the sections should be sharp at the keel, at least in the bow and the quarter. An external keel is also helpful in order to establish the desired grip on the water.

The round form gives soft movements in side waves, but

Fig. 44 The V-shape in a strong wind and waves

requires more skill in handling than any other form. The modern racing canoes run very fast in the waves and behave smoothly and beautifully. They are, however, so unstable that they are safe only for specialists. A beamy round-bottom canoe will behave like the U-shaped one in all wave conditions.

In the bow very full lines should be avoided below the WL, especially in rockerless boats. Deep V-shaped sections cleave the waves smoothly and a high flaring freeboard will prevent the bow from digging too deeply.

The aft body in the past was beamy and flat (motor-yacht shaped), but because of the yawing tendency in a following sea this shape is not popular today. Instead, a rather full form with a cross section comprising the V and the round shape is used. The freeboard aft should be low.

The sheerline in the touring Canadian canoe is curved intensely near the ends. This is due to the fact that the boat is open; if decked like the kayaks there would be no risk of becoming swamped. In the latter, water can get inside only through the cockpit and the kayak must be high and buoyant at its middle in order to keep dry when riding on the crest of a wave. A spray cover eliminates swamping, but can feel uncomfortable to the canoeist as to some degree it hampers his movements and very soon will cause damp and moisture inside the hull. A weak sheerline curve is accordingly preferable in kayaks—it also lessens the windage.

The wind drift is considerable in beamy, high-built canoes. Thus the touring Canadian will scarcely make any advance in a strong wind if paddled only by one person. The steering is also heavily affected and the rudderless Canadian will soon teach us what happens in a wind. By trimming the canoe low at the stern, it turns away from the wind and conversely it turns against the wind when trimmed low in the bow. When at speed, nearly all canoes tend to turn against that side from which the wind is blowing and, as has been shown, the remedy is a low aft body.

The stem and stern profile acts on the sections in such a manner that a vertical stem tends to narrowness below the WL, whereas a marked overhang makes for blunt sections. For this reason, and also to reduce the wind drift, exaggerations in overhang should be avoided.

SPEED

Naturally speed is a question of water resistance of which the main part—75-90 per cent—is caused simply by friction between hull and water. The highest percentage is found at the lowest speed.

The frictional resistance depends on the size and the condition of the surface below the WL and increases with the speed. A minimum of 'wetted surface' can be achieved in a short deep hull with sections of true semi-circular form below the WL. In order to keep them semi-circular all the way, however, a large amount of rocker must be added, otherwise the boat will draw too deep at the stem and stern and thus again add to the wetted surface. A boat such as this is never built, as its stability is nil and as length and rocker have other functions of opposite demands. An approximation to the semi-circular form, where $\frac{BWL}{DL}$ is 3·4-3·0 has proved most efficient and is common in the modern racing canoes. V and U shaped sections will increase the wetted surface about 5 and 2 per cent respectively.

With regard to the condition of the surface of the hull, absolute smoothness is essential and grains of dust or sand in the varnish must be avoided. A coat of wax, oil, soap, in order to reduce friction, is useless.

The remaining 10-25 per cent of the resistance represents the energy lost by the creation of waves at bow and stern. By the way, this lost energy may be picked up again—by another competitor 'hanging on the wave' of the canoe in front of him. This *wave resistance* is also called the form resistance because it depends upon the form of any boat. It has little effect at low speeds but as the hull moves more quickly it increases more rapidly than the frictional resistance. In fact, the difference in performance of two models is usually due to the amount of wave resistance. To reduce wave resistance, the best remedy is to increase the length followed by decreasing the beam and achieving a correct prismatic coefficient.

Any canoe can be propelled with a very small amount of effort until a speed of about 4 knots. Up to this point only the frictional resistance counts: the wave resistance is negligible. The bow wave is low and short and there is no marked hollow behind it (Fig. 45a).

Fig. 45   Wave resistance

Above 5-6 knots the wave resistance grows rapidly. The bow wave becomes heavy and so long that the stern drops in the hollow behind it (Fig. 45b). When the level rises again behind the canoe, the stern wave is superimposed on its top and the result is a smooth transverse wave usable for 'hanging'.

At about 8 knots the wave now stretches to the middle of the canoe where a big beam would heavily increase the disturbance of the water. The transverse wave is heavy and comes up far behind the canoe, ideal for 'hanging'. The change of trim is most marked at this speed (Fig. 45c).

Ten knots will bring the crest of the wave near to the middle of the boat and the heavy aft trim starts to decrease again (Fig. 45d). If there was power enough to make a further 3 knots, the canoe would plane in front of its own bow wave.

Regardless of the size of the boat the wave length depends only on the speed. Accordingly, the wave phenomena just mentioned will appear at higher speeds in each case if the boat becomes longer. For a 17-foot boat, 5·5 knots is called the 'squatting speed' where the unfavourable wave pattern begins to manifest itself. For a 21-foot boat, this will occur at one knot more speed. Another reason why length will pay is due to the lower waves produced when the displacement is spread over a long hull. A high PC (above 0·6) contributes to speed in the same way.

For planing, however, length is unfavourable. On the figures given the canoe was suggested to be 17 feet, whereas 12 feet would give planing conditions at 10 instead of 13 knots. Unfortunately, this speed is never achieved as the resistance at the lower speeds is too great in a 12-footer. Every imaginable experiment has been tried out, but the lack of horsepower is evident. Experience has proved the best performance to be with a form where the planing features were modified to such a degree that none of the other speed-making factors were affected. This is, however, a problem only in racing canoes.

The touring canoes never achieve this 'squatting speed' in their ordinary use.

MANŒUVRABILITY

Manœuvrability is the ability of a canoe to change its course quickly and is mostly required in inland canoeing. On lakes and easy rivers a normal touring canoe will serve well, but for rapid rivers, blocked more or less with rocks, a special type of canoe is necessary. In such 'white water canoes' and still more in the slalom canoes, the manœuvrability has been developed to its fullest extent. This is only possible at the expense of other aspects of performance. For a fast turn, a short hull with a small draught specially at the ends is essential. We have seen that such a form performs very badly in a seaway and the speed is also heavily affected.

The different demands of manœuvrability is dividing canoes into racing and open sea types with a long hull and a small amount of rocker, and the white water canoes of the opposite form, short hull and much rocker. Between these main groups a great many canoes of compromise form are found. Most of them are excellent for average conditions, but they should never be used for open sea, or white water canoeing.

A rudder is impracticable in a strong current, but it is very suitable for the directionally stable cruising and racing kayaks. The hinged stern rudder which is good for inland canoeing is unsuited for sea canoeing as in high waves it will occasionally be clear of the water. Here the fin rudder being attached one to two feet in front of the stern works perfectly, but it is liable to be easily damaged by obstructions in shallow water.

CANOE TYPES

Modern canoes are either the decked kayaks propelled with a double-bladed paddle, or Canadian canoes being open and single-bladed paddled. The kayaks are the faster and more seaworthy, but they require more skill in handling. In a Canadian canoe paddling is easily learnt and they are fairly stable and roomy. The kayak is primarily a single-seater, whereas the Canadian performs at its best as a double-seater.

The Touring Kayak

This developed from the Eskimo sealskin kayak which is still in use in Greenland and the arctic parts of Canada, Alaska and Siberia. Kayaks were first seen by Europeans when Greenland and Canada were discovered about the year 890. About 1450 some Greenland kayaks were shipped to Denmark and Norway and one was hanging in the dome of Trondheim for a long period. In 1801 a flotilla of kayakers was proposed to fight the British navy, but this plan was never realized—fortunately, you may say. During the last war British and Danish canoeists had the same enemy and in 1942 Lt-Col H. G. Hasler made his successful attack on ships in the port of Bordeaux.

About 1840 the first copies of Greenland kayaks appeared in Europe although in Hungary a domestic type at least 1,000 years old was still in existence. In our time the ancient European canoe types have completely disappeared, but copies of the Arctic ones are still built, mostly in the United Kingdom.

There are a great many types of Arctic kayaks, differing greatly from one place to another. The length can vary from 16 to more than 20 feet and the beam from 16 to 21 inches. The natives consider the long and narrow types as the most seaworthy. The chine form is due to the frame construction and the basic shape is typified by the narrow ends, where the longitudinal lines sometimes have concave curves.

As kayaks are used for fishing and hunting among ice floes manœuvrability is an important factor and consequently many kayaks, especially in sheltered water, are given a considerable amount of rocker. This further decreases the low PC and is the reason that most Greenland kayaks run easily only at low speeds.

The fore and aft sections are sharp at the keel and the chine, so that the kayak is not inclined to yaw very much. In this way manœuvrability is combined with seaworthiness. The latter is further improved by the long overhanging stem profiles which increase the buoyancy as well as the directional stability when immersed in the waves.

After 1865 canoeing began to rise as a new kind of sport. The Scot, McGregor, made his sensational voyages in kayaks of his own design. These Rob-Roys were more ship-shaped than the Arctic types. The basic form was a box-shaped middle part running into a moderately rounded V-shape in the bow and quarter sections.

The Rob-Roys were comparatively short and beamy, L:15 feet, B:28 inches, but because of the short overhang and the flat curve of rocker, they utilized their length better than the Arctic types. Primarily McGregor's kayaks were much more stable and they were also rather faster because of their better PC. In rough water the Arctic types performed better, but they required too much skill in handling to contribute much to the growth of canoeing. The Rob-Roy type spread to the continent, starting the sport of canoeing in many countries.

About 1910 a new shape appeared in Sweden, being adapted from the motor-yacht. The idea was to cleave the water vertically with a deep, narrow bow and let it leave again horizontally under a flat beamy quarter. This shape was claimed to be speedy and seaworthy at the same time, but the higher speed was gained from more length and less beam and not from the shape. When heading into the waves, these kayaks behaved excellently, but in a following sea they could scarcely be worse.

Today touring kayaks are again 'double ended', being only a little fuller aft than fore. The single-seater above 16 feet is faster and moves more smoothly in the waves than the 15-footer which, in turn, is less awash. In my opinion 24 inches gives a sufficient beam for the long types and one inch more is enough for the short one. The speed is normally 4·5–5·0 knots. The double-seater makes one knot more—L:17–19 feet, B:26–28 inches.

The details of the shape depend on the use and the demands of the individual and refer to the performance concerned. New features from the racing canoes like the narrow fore body must soon influence the touring kayaks as the greater freedom of movement is also of benefit to the touring canoeist.

The Touring Canadian Canoe

This type originated from the birch-bark canoes used by the Indians in North America. The prototypes may be divided into two groups: a river type with very high freeboard at the stem and stern, good for foamy rivers; and another type with a more moderately curved sheerline made for lakes and coastal waters. There the high type caused trouble in the wind. An approach was also made to the decked kayaks far north in Alaska and on the Aleutian Islands.

As might be expected, the first use of Canadian canoes for sport and pleasure was in their native countries—Canada and

U.S.A. Very soon boat-builders started producing them commercially and in Chicago hundreds of timber Canadian canoes had been built by 1881.

The touring Canadians cannot develop much without losing their special features, i.e., they should be open, beamy and possess the high arched stems. The basic form belongs to the ship-shape we noticed in the Rob-Roys.

The river canoe is so rockered that it will lose too much buoyancy near its ends if this is not compensated by means of full lines. Equipped with a full-length spray cover, this type is serviceable for very fast rivers, but it is tiring for the canoeist on a straight course.

The lake canoe is directionally stable by being rockerless and the deep stem sections require fineness to such an extent that the horizontal lines are usually concave near the ends. This must, however, not be exaggerated. Paddled by two persons, one in each end, the lake Canadian is sufficiently manœuvrable, also on rivers if they are not too fast.

For coastal canoeing bilge keels and a spray cover will to some degree increase the seaworthiness, but the kayak always performs much better, and is safer.

The great advantage of the Canadian is the practicability of sleeping in them. With a beam of 36 inches there is room enough for two persons, and a tent-like cover can easily be raised over a number of arched hoops extending partly or entirely the length of the canoe as preferred. The length of such a 'cabin-cruiser' should be about 16 feet—the river type 14–15 feet. The speed is approximately 3·5 knots (Fig. 46).

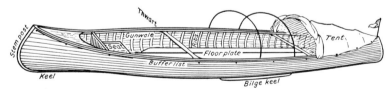

Fig. 46   The touring Canadian. In England the part designated as 'buffer list' is known as a 'rubbing strake'

The White Water Canoes

These are the rockered variants of the short touring types we have discussed already. They are usually built for racing in accordance with international rules. Besides manœuvrability and speed the stability is also an important factor so that they are used for touring as well. Some ability to keep the course is advantageous and this is the reason why many canoeists prefer the old folding boats where the chines offer steadiness. This, however, has gradually been achieved in the glass-fibre boats by means of slightly deeper and more V-shaped sections fore and aft. Softly curved stem profiles prevent damage from obstructions in the water. Many models are surprisingly low at the bow so that the water first flows away near the cockpit where the deck is raised to a considerable height. A moderately curved sheerline, combined with a more horizontal shape of the deck, would certainly perform better.

The Slalom Canoes
Slalom canoes are so specialized that it is difficult to maintain a straight course on them. They react immediately to the paddle strokes on any direction desired, even sideways. They are shorter than 14 feet, being narrower and more rockered than the white water canoes. Consequently, unusually full lines are essential and they are nowadays worked into the hull and the deck as well. In order not to touch the hanging poles of the slalom gates, the boats are very low built. The rocker is curved most intensively near the ends running smoothly to the stem heads. The sections are round, or U-shaped.

The Racing Canoes
Canoe racing started between 1860 and 1870 and for many years each country used its own type, Greenland kayaks, custom types, or Rob-Roys. Racing shells from the rowing sport were also used, but about 1910 the motor-yacht-shaped type of Swedish design began to spread. The measurements from these kayaks were used for the rules when the International Canoe Federation started in 1924. In the 1930s the fish-shape was dominant for some years and then there was a change to more symmetrical hulls. The sections changed from U to V and narrow unstable boats appeared first on kayaks and then also within the Canadian type. In 1956 concave sections were introduced in order to reduce the WL-beam. This was possible already by means of the V-shape, especially if the canoes were high built, but low hulls with round sections provided a better solution. In the round form the wetted surface is smaller, but the hull much beamier. Concave sections or high flaring freeboards make it possible to decrease the beam and while concavity was banned from 1963 the other remedy is still legal (Fig. 41).

Today, freedom for movement during the paddle strokes grows more and more important due to the advances in paddling technique. Consequently, the widest point of the canoes is located so far aft that they are very narrow at their bow and middle part. At the widest point the freeboard is so high that the width can be worked away above the WL. The narrow bow develops until there is just room enough for the canoeist. Unfortunately, the speed in rough water and even also in calm water is affected by this. The PC tends to be too low, planing effect no longer exists and the buoyancy is kept within a larger wetted surface than before. The solution to this problem is to add buoyancy to the bow below the gunwale, and at the same time to keep the narrowness where it is advantageous to the paddle work. In the latest canoes the bow sections are continuing edgeless into the deck and the arched freeboards are deflecting the bow wave much better than the earlier vertical ones (Fig. 47).

Fig. 47   Modifications to the racing canoe

In racing canoes only the speed counts, but as speed also includes rough water performance, seaworthiness comes into consideration. Due to the high speed and the long narrow hull, racing canoes cut through the waves rather than climb over them. In rough water they are almost constantly awash and even in the wake from competitors the deck occasionally cleaves the water. To avoid this, we need extremely high free-boards but as the wind resistance must be the lowest possible they have never been introduced. Instead, the shape of the deck is modified and slalom and racing canoes have found buoyant deck sections and edgeless gunwales.

The racing kayaks include K1, K2 and K4. Earlier the size of wetted surface was considered as being nearly fixed and almost impossible to bring down. Nevertheless, it has decreased about

6 per cent compared with the 1950 boats. The remedy was round narrow sections, $\dfrac{\text{BWL}}{\text{DWL}}$ being 3·0–3·2. A still narrower and deeper section is too unstable and has proved no advantage in speed. Rocker generally decreases the wetted surface but increases the change of trim. A rocker line being flat at its middle and curved more and more intensively towards the ends provides the best results. The K1 is specially sensitive to changes in the rocker—a quarter of an inch can be felt in performance. Too much makes the kayak bounce in the spurts, and too little makes it feel 'dead' and harsh running over the racing distances.

Planing features such as deep and flat aft sections are efficient only to a smooth paddling style. In the latest K1 and K2 planing forms only exist in so far as the centre of buoyancy is worked deeper in the hull towards the stern, i.e., the bow has fuller form above the WL and the quarter is fuller in or below the WL. This does not agree with the modern narrow form unless we use the arched freeboards previously mentioned. In a K4 no planing or lifting effect is possible: here the frictional resistance is still more important than in the K1 and K2.

K1—L. (max.) 520 cm., B. (min.) 51 cm., Weight (min.). 12 kg. Highest speed: 10,000 m. 7·2 knots: 1,000 m. 8·2 kn.: 500 m. 8·8 kn.: Spurts 10.0kn.

K2—L. (max.) 650 cm., B. (min.) 55 cm., Weight (min.) 18 kg. Speed: 10,000 m. 7·8 kn.: 1,000 m. 8·9 kn.: 500 m. 9·7 kn.: Spurts 11·5 kn.

K4—L. (max.) 1,100 cm., B. (min.) 60 cm., Weight (min.) 30 kg. Speed: 10,000 m. 8·6 kn.: 1,000 m. 10·0 kn.: 500 m. 10·8 kn.

The racing Canadian canoes C1 and C2 began developing later than the kayaks, but then continued until they had not the slightest likeness with traditional Canadian canoes. All that is left is the Canadian beam of 75 cm. being located like a sort of rudiment far aft and high above the WL. In my opinion, the Canadian canoe should never have been the prototype for single-bladed paddling. Look at the overgrown C8 being 3 feet wide, and compare it with the low and narrow South Sea war canoe! In a racing single canoe 75 cm. is also an enormous width, only doing harm to the steering. The beam can be measured anywhere on the canoe and so it only influences the gunwale shape, whereas below the WL the canoes are exactly as narrow as the kayaks. They only differ by being rockerless and in that a small amount of V-shape is often added to the bottom of the round sections, especially in the quarter. Even if this means a larger wetted surface the directional stability gained is essential to the steering. Turns are made by leaning the canoe. The height at the widest point is necessary for this reason as well as to get a small WL beam. If not counterbalanced by means of a very low stern, this height makes for trouble in steering with the wind on the side.

C1—L. (max.) 520 cm., B. (min.) 75 cm., Weight (min.) 16 kg. Speed: 10,000 m. 6·0 kn.: 1,000 m. 7·2 kn.: 500 m. 7·8 kn.

C2—L. (max.) 650 cm., B. (min.) 75 cm., Weight (min.) 20 kg. Speed: 10,000 m. 7·0 kn.: 1,000 m. 8·1 kn.: 500 m. 8·6 kn.

C8 (not accepted for international championships)—L. (max.) 1,100 cm., B. (min.) 93 cm. The speed is nearly that of a K1.

A rudder is legal on kayaks whereas no kind of steering mechanism is allowed in Canadians. If fitted, an external keel shall be straight and the two halves of any cross section when divided by a vertical centre line shall be symmetrical. The deck, if any, shall leave 295 cm. free of a C1 and C2 regardless.

10

Canoe Building

ALAN BYDE

In 1972, the BBC presented a television series called 'Canoe'; programmes 6 and 7 showed canoe construction. The producer and I wrote a duplicated handout between us. We expected to send out about 500–800 altogether. In the first ten days 1,650 were sent out, and requests were still coming in. I provided the material for the piece, but the producer re-wrote it. Here is an extract:

'Methods of Construction
Early canoes were carved from the solid—from the simple dug-out to the huge Maori war canoe driven by 60 paddlers.

'Primitive man used framework canoes with coverings of hide or birch bark.

'Then came planked canoes, starting with the clinker built Rob Roy canoe of 1860.

'This method was gradually superseded by rigid and collapsible canoes made of proofed canvas stretched over a framework.

'Plywood provided an alternative covering; the Danes produce beautiful hot-moulded veneer canoes which are the ultimate for racing. Cold moulding is also used.

'Early in the 1960's came the revolution of glass fibre (glass reinforced plastic, known as grp). This has almost replaced other methods because of its simplicity, cheapness, strength, and good looks.

'Other current methods include plywood cut and stitched into shape (with or without formers), sometimes reinforced by grp.

'Our programme concentrated on grp construction. These notes will do the same.'

Quote ends. If I tried for a year I couldn't produce a more succint statement than that. This chapter now concentrates exclusively on grp canoe construction.

The basic stages in constructing a canoe in grp, working from the idea to the reality, go as follows:

1. Designer's experience   10 years
2. Drawing plans, calculations   10 hours
3. Making pattern, known as the plug   20 hours
4. Filling and polishing plug   100 hours
5. Mould building   20 hours
6. Making the canoe   10 hours
7. Ideas feedback from design in use   2 years
8. Improved model—back to square one.

This chapter will try to sketch the outlines of how to do it. A great deal must be assumed. It would need a whole book to treat the subject in detail, so I will concentrate on the bits the others do not tell.

DESIGNERS' EXPERIENCE

You need the ability to draw accurately on squared paper, to work out volumes from line drawing, to equate volumes of displaced water to carrying capacity at that displacement. Then you need a pattern-maker's skill, and they charge £2 an hour at current rates. A long history of patient bodging is my passport to this advanced condition. I suggest that a good bodger who has suffered through many sad errors and has still arisen to make more mistakes is a very valuable man. He understands many of the silly things that people do and how they drop into that series of cumulative errors. The craftsman, apprentice trained, has a healthy disrespect for the amateur, based on his own well-trained knowledge. Never be 'put down'. Your ideas, if they are worth more than a tinker's curse, are worth suffering with and through. Those who are going to do it are doing it. Those who are talking about it are not doing it. Have faith in your skill, or willingness to obtain it, be ready to suffer for it both in body and mind, but be sure to succeed.

Then you need to be able to pick up ideas, preferably from a car body worker, who is skilled in taking the kinks out of bent motors. He knows which tools to use, how to use them, and how to eradicate those two bogies—ripples and flats. Fortunately in Oxford we have motor works and young men from those works come to the Centre of which I am Warden. They educate me.

Finally, know your canoes. Look at commercial canoes, build a few dozen (I must have built hundreds now); and use them in the surf, in the roaring white water, way out on the sunbaked seas, in swimming pools, and on canals. There is no beginning and no end. Just start.

How to start? Join a canoe club, or write to the British Canoe Union, 26–29 Park Crescent, London W1N 4DT. You may even write to me (51 Ramsay Road, Headington, Oxford) but please enclose a stamped addressed return envelope, 4 x 9 inches, because my replies sometimes require lots of paper and drawings.

DRAWING PLANS

MATERIALS REQUIRED

Three sheets of paper, 20 x 30 inches, squared in tenths. I use imperial measure, but some prefer to use metric squared paper.

Drawing pen and black drawing ink.

Ruler with suitable divisions (metric or imperial)

Flexible curve

Pencils, 2H, sharpener, eraser.

Tracing paper, two sheets 20 x 30 inches.

'Letraset' or stencil system for lettering drawings.

You can use a square if you like—I never do, I use the squared paper.

DESIGN METHOD

Take one sheet of squared paper. This is the rough work sheet. Decide the length and beam and depth of your boat. The following guide should help:

Solo slalom kayak	LOA 13 ft 6 ins; Beam 24 ins; Depth 11 ins.
Solo white-water kayak	LOA 15 ft; Beam 24 ins; Depth 12 ins.
Solo sea kayak	LOA 16 ft 6 ins–18 ft; Beam 20–22 ins; Depth 12 ins.
Solo touring kayak	LOA 14 ft; Beam 24 ins; Depth 12 ins.
Double touring kayak	LOA 17 ft; Beam 27 ins; Depth 12½ ins.

These are a few of the popular sizes on which to base your

calculations. Now, mark out along the top of the sheet, on a scale of 1–10, the length overall (LOA) and beam of the boat and draw the profile first. Sketch this in with a soft pencil, say HB. Decide from experience whether you want a lot of rocker (for manœuvrability) or little (for speed); a deep bow section (for lift in heavy weather) or a pointed end (for reduced drag and side pressure when turning). When all these matters have been decided, when you know where you are going to put the cockpit, then go away and think about it for a week and then come back, rub it all out, and do it again. It's easy to rub out a light pencil line. Try rubbing out a chunk of construction fifteen-feet long, two-feet wide and a foot deep.

Having decided the profile, then draw the plan view. You need two sets of lines, the maximum beam line and the waterline. These must harmonize, for one line sets limitations upon a line near to it. Having decided these, take a scale cross-section at the point of maximum beam. This is only an idea, and has little relationship to what you do turn out in fact. However, it starts to concentrate your thinking on what you want. Again, design and experience come into it. Jorgen Samson in Chapter 9 is helpful in guiding one's thoughts. Most slalom kayaks are stern turning; that is, the bows tend to stay on a line but the back end slides out on a turn. A new idea is the bow turning slalom kayak where the stern trails in line with the boat, but the bows can be swung easily to point at their destination. Each has advantages. A stern turning boat will be flatter behind the cockpit and more vee'd in front underneath. The bow turning boat is the opposite. A vee bottom chine boat is usually a good sea boat. A round bottomed boat has minimum wetted area, and is usually built for speed but lacks stability. But remember, these are generalizations and success will depend upon the total harmony of line.

Take the second sheet of squared paper and mark out a centre vertical line and a base line, an inch above the bottom of the sheet. The horizontal axis should be in proportion to the length of the boat. I find that a fifteen-foot boat fits on to a thirty-inch sheet of paper if the horizontal scale is reduced to one to six. The vertical scale represents the total depth of the boat also half the beam, full size.

Using roughly estimated offsets from the outline sketch, transfer these to the axis arrangement on the second sheet. Dot in one line at a time. You are magnifying the horizontal and

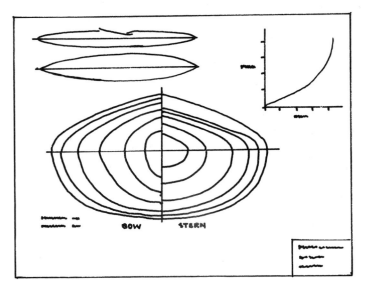

Fig. 48 Drawing—Finished Appearance

vertical offsets by ten, so all errors will also be magnified by ten. This shows in irregular lines when linking the dots. The line must be smoothed out, and I use the flexible curve to do this. The order in which I draw the lines, all on the same sheet, is as follows:

1. Profile (bow on left of sheet), including:
   Deck line
   Bow Rocker
   Planned waterline
2. Profile (stern on right of sheet), including:
   Deck line
   Stern rocker
   Planned waterline (same as for bow)
3. Plan (bow on left of sheet), including:
   Gunwale line
   Waterline
   Centre line
4. Plan (stern on right of sheet), including:
   Gunwale line
   Waterline
   Centre line

5. Station points. Draw at right angles to the horizontal base a series of vertical lines parallel to each other. The horizontal separation between them is called the common interval. On the drawing this is in scale. I use one-foot intervals on the boat, two-inch intervals on the drawing. Where each of these station lines crosses one of the lines already drawn, then a series of crossing points is established in two planes.

6. Master section. Take the third sheet of paper. The master section is drawn full size. It is only necessary to draw half of it as it is symmetrical about the vertical axis. However, if bow and stern sections are not symmetrical about the transverse axis drawn through the widest point of the canoe, then it is necessary to draw the bow half-sections on one side of the central axis and the stern half-sections on the other side.

The master section is at the widest point of the canoe on the plan. From it one derives the lines which build up all the other sections. It will be necessary at this point to check the master section against the lines obtained as above (1–5), and it may be necessary to modify them. This in turn leads to modifications of the master section. When these harmonizing efforts have been completed, then the rest of the sections may be drawn, harmonizing in turn with the master section.

To apply this in practice, set up axes at right angles as before. By patient work taking one station line at a time and by dotting in the crossing points, each sections shape can be determined at eight places as follows:

1. Deck line, centre
2. Gunwale line, right
3. Waterline, right
4. Rocker line
5, 6, 7, & 8. Other side, symmetrical with the first side.

The final series of sections is now complete. The lines are probably confused and messy. Take the drawing pen and the flexible curve, and taking each line in turn, draw it in boldly and finally. It must be correct. The only firm lines needed are the sections and the 1:10 scale plan and profile. Take the tracing paper and clip it on to the drawing board and arrange the inked-in drawing underneath to place the lines where they are wanted. Trace through using the flexible curve and the drawing pen, and finally tidy up the drawing with a border and information as to who drew it and when. Take the finished tracing to a copier, and have three copies run off: one for your files, one for the workshop, and one to show people.

It lends power to your drawings if you can calculate the volumes, and therefore the displacements, at three arbitrarily selected waterlines. Areas and volumes can be calculated with sufficient accuracy by judicious straightening of curves where necessary (Fig. 49). With three calculated points and origin on

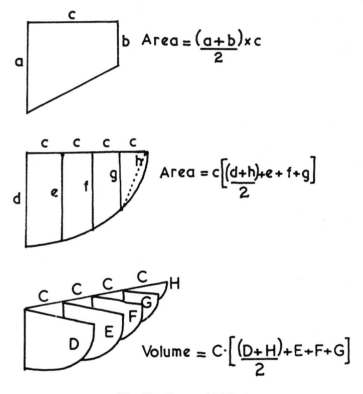

$$\text{Area} = \frac{(a+b) \times c}{2}$$

$$\text{Area} = c\left[\frac{(d+h)}{2} + e + f + g\right]$$

$$\text{Volume} = C \cdot \left[\frac{(D+H)}{2} + E + F + G\right]$$

Fig. 49 Trapezoidal Rule

a graph, showing inches of draft horizontally against total displacement vertically, then the optimum waterline can be shown with the load that the canoe will carry at that waterline. Remember to allow for the weight of the canoe itself. At this point, if you find that you have a waterline of four inches draft on a solo slalom kayak and a calculated load of 600 pounds, then you can be sure that you have designed a freak, or that your calculations are wrong. For this type of canoe, a four-inch draft should give about 180—200 pounds loading. Alternatively, if you have designed a touring double for adults and the load waterline is four inches with a load of 280 pounds, you have boobed again. You need more carrying capacity than for two people each weighing ten stone in a touring double.

PLUG, OR PATTERN, MAKING

Take a copy of your drawing to the workshop. You will also need:

1. $\frac{1}{2}$-inch blockboard, or plywood, for section shapes, say 4 foot by 4 foot
2. Carbon paper, pencil, or ball point.
3. Power jig saw (I use a Black and Decker 850 two speed drill).
4. Clamps, benches, usual workshop tools for wood working.
5. A spine, or building board, for the boat. This should be top quality knot-free redwood, 3 inches, planed, and the length of the boat.
6. Large quantity of heavy cardboard, (i.e. from a supermarket scrap heap).
7. Industrial stapling gun and 5,000 staples.

Trace the sections, one at a time, on to the plywood or blockboard. Allow a thickness of about $\frac{3}{4}$ x $\frac{1}{4}$ inches for the skin of the plug. Cut square holes centrally on each of the section shapes and slot them in order on to the spine. Pin each section into place on the spine with panel pins each side of it. Pull four cords tightly from end to end of the plug, one along the keel line, one along the deck line, and one along each gunwale line. Staple across them into the edge of the sections after suitable adjustments have been made. This anchors the sections and stops wobble. You can use drilled and screwed stringers cut into slots if you like, but I'm working as an ace bodger who gets results in a hurry.

Take the cardboard sheets and offer them up to the plug carcass. Mark off, cut with Stanley trimming knife, or similar, and staple into place. Cover the whole skeleton structure. It doesn't matter if you have gaps, or even if you have lumps on it at this stage—although humps should be reduced if possible.

Now, coat the whole horrible cardboard shape with one layer of $1\frac{1}{2}$-ounce glass mat well stippled down. The cardboard may not take heavy rolling at this stage, so stippling with the brush is required. Work on the deck first and then on the hull. Leave it for a day to set hard enough to cut. At this stage the glassed over plug is rough and shaggy, has some lumps and many hollows and flats on it. Use the disc sander. I use a Black and Decker two speed drill on top speed with a 6-inch heavy duty sanding disc in it, such as the motor works use. The fancy paper-backed discs which you get at hardware shops will not do. Cut down the humps, perhaps right through the carcass leaving a few holes rough-edged with cardboard. If this happens, tape over with heavy masking tape, 2 inches wide. Now re-skin the whole carcass with its second layer of 1½-ounce glass mat. I use up all the odd bits of rubbishy glass in my 'bits bin' at the end of the glass table. After this skin has hardened, cut down the humps and bumps, and perhaps fill in odd hollows with extra layers of glass and resin. Patch over any holes which still show, or any thin parts that flex too easily. Now, if you want to be really sure of the carcass, skin it once again with 1½-ounce glass mat and laminating resin.

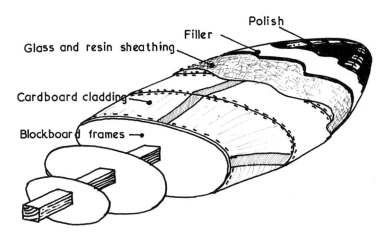

Fig. 50   Bat 5 Plug

After all this you should have a fairly accurate shape which bears some resemblance to the original idea. Be prepared for some surprises as the lines develop in the shaping. Remember also that a pattern maker would be reduced to tears by this approach, but ace bodging baffles brains. It is the finished polished skin that matters. If the substructure is strong enough for one copy to be made, that is enough.

PLUG FILLING AND POLISHING

It is now necessary to fill the surface of the plug to the approximate designed skin shape. I used to use a self-made mix of laminating resin and chalk powder, or slate powder, both very cheap and both making rather hard surfaces which require hours of dusty, dirty cutting down. Don't do it. It's not worth the work. Buy a 16-pound tin of David's Isopon P38 filler, from the motor trade people, cost about £3 trade price.

Put the rough glassed plug on the trestles. Work all over it, mixing about half a pound of filler at a time, and remembering that it goes off in ten minutes in a warm atmosphere, filling all the little hollows, and generally wiping the filler as level as possible all over the part of the plug you can see. Keep at it until the whole plug is covered—maybe very roughly, but covered. When the whole thing is hard, probably as soon as you have finished wiping on the fourth mix of filler, return to the first area covered and cut down with a motor body cutting tool, some call it a dreadnought file: I prefer a blade from a tool by Aven which takes a flexible but brittle blade about 14 inches long. I use a fresh blade for each new plug. The wiping process will have left ridges in the filler which will set hard. Cut within an hour and you will find the material cuts easily, but after a day it is less easy. This hand cutting is essential at this stage in order to get all the high spots out. Ignore the low spots, they will fill up anyway. DO NOT UNDER ANY CIRCUMSTANCES USE A DISC SANDER AT THIS STAGE. This is how the amateur put ripples into his boat, because the disc sander is too inaccurate.

Fill all over once again. If it is a big boat with many hollows because your cardboard plug was too uneven, then you will possibly need another tin of filler. After the second filling, you should spend at least ten hours cutting and cutting again with the hand tools. YOU MUST NOT USE THE DISC. This hand cutting is tedious and tiring, but a canoeist's shoulders are strong and fit and the steady swing of the hands and the tool held in them is soon acquired. The whole body should enter into the steady swing. Some music helps, I find. Now when you are more or less satisfied, go over the pale-grey filled plug with a distant spot of light, looking for highlights and hollows and slight ridges. Mark these with a felt pen. Just draw a ring around each hollow or fault spotted. With a little filler at a time, fill the small hollows still left. Be very selective, and wipe off level with great care. Brood over it.

Then, when the third filling has hardened, cut down all over again—this takes at least ten hours. I find that is about two days with other jobs fitted in when I get bored stiff. Refill any deep scratches or grooves, or even, as the highlights start to appear, rebuild some flat area, layer upon layer until that area harmonizes with the surrounding areas. The palm of the hand brushed lightly over the surface is the most accurate tell-tale of irregular surfaces that you have, surprisingly it is more sensitive than the eye.

The plug is now roughly finished, and all the ripples and flats should be out of it. It is all done with steel tools in cutting up to this point.

Polishing

Use 60-grade 'Production Paper'—I buy this in 25-sheet quires from the motor supply people. Fit a quarter sheet around a hard cabinet maker's sanding block, and sand away meticulously all over. The various cuts and scrapes of the steel tools will start to vanish. You will find a few tiny hollows to fill and this must be done. Don't try to sand fresh filler, this will only clog the paper: allow 6 to 24 hours drying time. At the end of this stage the surface will be even and smooth, but dull and powdery to look at.

Now put on four layers of 'Furane' resin, a special resin made for this purpose. It is like water, and brown when applied. It is very inflammable. I wear gloves for this job as the resin stains the hands, and some say that the material is carcinogenous, but I am not sure about that. Anyway, take great care with it. Each layer can go on about half-an-hour after the preceding layer. Leave it to harden for twenty-four hours. The thin brown resin will harden to jet black with a fine but unpolished hard surface.

Take 180-grade wet-and-dry cutting paper and use it wet, wrapped around a hard cabinet maker's sanding block. Sand all over, cutting down in some cases to the grey filler layers underneath the 'Furane' layer. Some more filling may be necessary after this process has dried and been dusted off. A fair polish should now show, and a distant spot of light will pick out highlights very effectively, thus indicating ripples and flats.

After satisfying yourself that the surface is as flat and as near perfect as you can get it, coat any white areas with 'Furane', allow to dry, and then give the whole boat two or more coats of 'Furane'. Leave to harden for a day or even two. Then, using the hard sanding block with 360-grade wet-and-dry cutting paper, rub down thoroughly all over. Try not to cut down into the filler layers beneath the 'Furane'. Using a soft rubber sanding block and 600-grade wet-and-dry paper, rub down all over again. The surface should now have a dull shine on it.

At this point the brackets of the trestles should be well padded with clean padding bound with tape, otherwise the high polish required will be marked by dirt on the trestle arms. Obtain a polishing mop for the power hand drill. I use a 5-inch mop about an inch thick. I also use a cutting and glazing compound sold by Valley Canoe Products. It is imported from U.S.A. and is expensive, but very good. This is smeared on with a cloth, then the mop is used to cut the top surface of the resin. I once used a very heavy industrial sander and at 10,000 revs. it simply whipped the top surface of the 'Furane' away in a flash. Very sad, that was. The handyman drill we have runs at 2,400 revs. and that is about right. Polish with the mop twice all over. The plug should now have a really glossy finish, and a rub over with a dry cloth will bring a high shine to it. Now is the time when the final highlight check shows all the little ripples you didn't see before, and all the flats which need filling. Don't bother. If the boat is successful, later plugs and moulds will correct these minor flaws. If it isn't successful, then it's not worth bothering with anyway.

Start the final polishing. Each layer of high quality polish should be put on by hand not closer than six hours apart, and preferably a day apart. Six clear polishings are required. I use a polish called 'Mirrorglaze' or an American polish from Valley Canoe Products. Both are expensive. Some people use 'Simoniz' and say this is good, but I have no experience with it. Car body finishers use a special polish with a cutting paste in it just before the final polishing, but I haven't obtained any of this yet.

At this stage one regards all people who enter the workshop with grave suspicion. It only needs one scratch with a sharp edge and the polish is spoiled.

MOULD BUILDING

First of all a temporary flange must be set up against the boat. The simplest way is to use a hardboard flange fitted to the boat with alloy tabs fixed with self-tapping screws, but this type of flange has a sway-backed look to it. It is all right for amateur boats when any boat is a joy to have, but professionals will not accept a swaying joint line—it is not good enough for them. I once spent a great deal of time getting the flange right, and then a manufacturer took it, sighed, made a plug from my moulds, and then set off and put his own flange on to his own requirements. Now I don't bother so much, and the manufacturer can please himself.

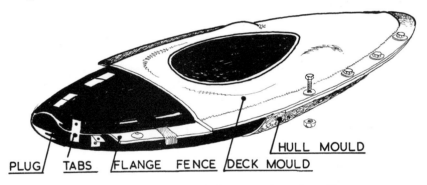

PLUG   TABS   FLANGE   FENCE   DECK MOULD   HULL MOULD

Fig. 51   Bat 5: Method of construction of moulds

After the temporary flange has been fitted, the screw heads are covered with sticky tape, as are the joints in the hardboard sections. The gap between the plug and the flange is taped over underneath on the bracket side of the flange. The remaining gap is then filled with cheap mould wax or with 'Plasticene', and smoothed level with a palette knife.

The flange is waxed twice, and the plug surface is again polished. The whole surface must be polished dry. Then it is coated with release agent spread very, very thinly using a soft sponge to mop it on and taking great care that every bit of surface is coated. When this has dried, the whole surface is covered with a layer of gelcoat and when this has hardened the flanges are built up using 1½-ounce chopped strand mat. I find that trying to span the gap between the plug and the flange in one go is impossible, as it leaves air gaps around the flange edge and the resin edge is too thick and brittle in use. Keep the resin thin around the joint line. Some mould builders run a long string, or two, of rovings into this corner so that dense fibrous re-inforcement is obtained. The flanges should have two layers laid flat on to them, one layer up the side of the plug, then one layer to span the gap. The whole exposed surface of the plug is now coated with three layers of $1\frac{1}{2}$-ounce mat. Sometimes it may be necessary to build a re-inforcing rib around the cockpit in order to strengthen it.

When the resin has gelled, the waste material at the flange edge is trimmed to the temporary fence. When the whole lot is well set and fairly hard, say next day, turn the plug and half mould, remove the anchoring screws, and pry the temporary fence away. The screw holes are filled with wax and the remaining

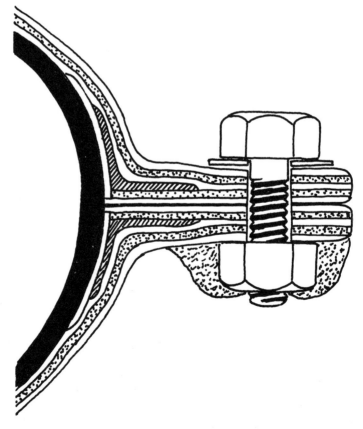

Fig. 52 Mould flange

plasticene, or wax, is scraped out of the joint line. Then the whole flange is waxed twice and the plug once, and after the release agent has dried the other half of the mould is cast. When both halves have been cast and roughly trimmed, leave to harden for a day. Mark off where the fastenings are to go. I use trapped nuts spaced about 12 inches apart. I used to use mould keys, but I found that amateur builders often failed to clean out the keys properly, and the accumulating resin forced the flanges apart and so spoilt the joint line. Now, I advise that flat flanges with trapped nuts are better as they are easier to clean.

The $\frac{1}{4}$-inch Whitworth bolts and nuts are lightly greased and put into the $\frac{1}{4}$-inch diameter holes that have been drilled. Tighten the nuts up, and ensure that the bolt heads have good wide washers under them. Turn the mould with the plug in it, nut side uppermost. Mix about a quarter of a pound of gelcoat resin and a quantity of glass mat scraps to make a dough. Form blocks of this dough around each of the nuts in turn, using the fingers, and leave to harden for a day.

Remove the bolts from their holes—they will come out quite easily even with resin on the threads, as the bolt simply screws out of the threaded resin around it. Using a bricklayer's bolster, start to lever the flanges apart. To assist the separation, thump the mould surface with the fist, nothing harder or heavier. Eventually the mould shells should separate. If they don't, it is stuck, and you are in trouble. It happened to me last week, through trying to hurry a new set of moulds through the polishing in three days. Unless you have a complete skin of wax between the plug and the mould the two components will bond together with disastrous results. So beware.

Take the plug and keep it handy for a week or two. When the moulds are producing and you have made another plug from the new moulds, then you can destroy the original plug as it has served its purpose.

Master Plugs and Moulds

An amateur with just one set of moulds may think ahead a year or so, and wonder what will happen if his canoe is successful. For example, I built a baths trainer, known as the BAT. It was built as an exercise for a teacher's group in Wolverhampton and was started on 11th January, 1967. I didn't take a master plug out of the first set of moulds. The Mark 1 was not very good, but the Mark 2 took shape in August 1967. If I had known what the BAT was to become I would have framed the first one. Therefore, my advice is, as soon as you have taken out two or three canoes from a set of moulds and the moulds are well 'run in', then take out a slightly heavier canoe, coloured black or some dark colour in order to show up the highlights. Sling it up out of the way, polish it once in a while, and then later if you need to copy the moulds it is easy, and the shape is correct, undistorted by the punishment the average amateur building group gives to a set of moulds.

A manufacturer will make a master mould. This is in fact an inside-out half mould, rather like half the canoe with a flange attached. This master mould simplifies the business of copying the moulds, and can be kept in really good condition by the manufacturer.

After a while, if you have decided that the canoe you have made is a failure, then the plug can be made into a canoe; or if it is a success, then you can incorporate any modifications into your plug and use it as the basis for the Mark 2 model.

MAKING A CANOE

My best advice is to obtain the various booklets published. I know of the following.
1. BCU handbook on grp construction.
2. Trylon handbook.
3. Streamlyte handbook.
4. Strand Glass handbook.
5. Prima handbook.

There may be others, it's worth asking around. My book *Living Canoeing* has a chapter in detail on the subject.

The suggestion that you should look elsewhere for details of actually making the canoe will probably have reduced the earnest seeker after knowledge to impotent rage. I wish I could put it all in here, but there isn't room and so I have included the bits the others leave out and concentrated on those aspects which I know from experience need particular attention. Here are some more useful tips:
1. Use empty gallon polythene jars with the tops cut off as mixing pots. Half-gallon pots do just as well. An inch of resin in the gallon size equals a pound weight—near enough.

2. Extension brush for the joining strip. Use the horizontal alloy pole from the old-fashioned TV aerial. These can be had for a few pence from scrapyards. About 5 feet long is right. Wooden poles are either rigid but too heavy, or light enough but insufficiently rigid. The brush should be pushed into the end of the alloy TV pole which may need to be slightly flattened in a vice.

3. Very good longitudinal stiffeners can be made using a 12-foot length of alloy angle, 1 inch across flanges, $\frac{1}{8}$-inch thick, as a mould. Polish inside, lay up stiffener former, then use the cast former in the canoe under a single layer of mat. The alloy is not used in the boat, it is simply a mould.

4. Various patterns of rollers exist. I find the following types best for my purposes, remembering that amateurs tend not to look after tools as well as they should; and that good tools are more expensive to replace if rendered useless by solidified resin Woollen surface roller—'Handirolla' from Woolworths. Hard roller—the most expensive is better here. A paddle type is recommended. I suggest a large diameter one (2-inch) by Trylon or Prima, and a $\frac{3}{4}$-inch one from Prima. Washer types are cheaper, but I find them hopeless in use. Strand Glass has a good long roller, 4 inches, 1-inch diameter, ribbed, and easy to clean. Rollers are also obtainable from K & C Mouldings.

5. Polystyrene foam buoyancy blocks come from insulation suppliers, usually in blocks 3 feet by 2 feet by 3 inches. Cost for five such blocks is about £2 from the manufacturers— builders merchants will charge more. One such block cut in half, and then each half cut into two pieces; one piece shaped to fit the rear of the canoe directly behind the cockpit, and the other just in front of the footrest will give the canoe quite enough buoyancy for average river use.

6. Without any doubt, toggles for the canoe ends are better than loops, and Valley Canoe Products supply them either direct or through other suppliers.

7. A fail-safe footrest is essential if a footrest is used. Tyne Canoes have a good one which is easy to adjust but difficult to build as it requires special alloy sheet pressings as side plates. Valley Canoe Products have a very good one which is less easy to adjust, but which is easy to build in, or to adapt for existing canoes.

8. If, like me, you are responsible for a workshop used by young people, or anyone else for that matter, then do be sure

that before anybody enters that workshop you have pointed out the large notice warning them of the dangers in using resins and cleaners which are very inflammable. This notice is a 'life-saver' professionally. I also assume that suitable fire extinguishers have been installed, and that the fire officer for the area has been informed. We had our fire on the 11th December, 1970. I'll never forget that one. Workshop discipline really improved after that as people realised that the stuff *is* inflammable.

9. A copious supply of clean rags is needed, and disposal of rubbish can be difficult. Either you burn it locally and incur the displeasure of local residents, because the smoke is thick and black, or you put it in bins and the rubbish wagon takes it away, and that pollutes the ground eventually. If you make over sixty canoes a year, as we did last year, this becomes a real problem.

10. A source of warmth for the workshop is essential. The best thing we have used so far is a 2 kw. fan heater. If this is on a long lead, it can be put into a cockpit in order to persuade some flange fitting to 'go off' in a hurry, for example. I make little tents using an extension rod and some plastic sheeting to cover over something that needs to be cured in a hurry. The heater sucks in air from outside and blows hot air into the 'tent'. Ten minutes of this will send anything off—provided it has been catalysed. How to worry someone who is finding resin slow to 'go off'. Ask 'Did you put catalyst in?' And they always reply with scorn, 'Of course.' And a minute later they have that indrawn thoughtful expression.

11. If you have setting problems, typically a layer of gelcoat in a mould which has not gone off by next day, then you *know* it hasn't been mixed with catalyst, despite the earnest protestations to the contrary by the lads who did it. (They all do; protest, I mean). Then mix about a quarter pint of brush cleaner with about 100 cc. of catalyst, and bush lightly all over the wet gelcoat surface. The cleaner spreads the catalyst evenly, and evaporates in a minute or two. The catalyst then leaches down into the resin and starts it going off. If the gelcoat is very thick it may not penetrate enough, so it will be necessary to 'stir' the gelcoat on the mould surface with catalyst after it has been spread. Leave for half a day if possible, and it should then be quite hard enough.

12. Brush cleaning is easy if you follow the rules:

    a. Make a big fuss about your own brush. I call mine

'Byde's brush', and it is better quality than the others. I write 'Byde's brush' on the handle in black marker pen ink. This mystique about *the* brush, plus a few histrionics now and then, makes everyone rather brush conscious and it really does help to keep the brushes clean. And, if you look after the brushes, the boat will look after itself.

    b. Squeeze resin out of the brush in the brush cleaner. Usually the cleaner is soggy with resin. If the brush has started to solidify, you can catch it when rubbery by bashing the brush bristles with a hammer, and then cleaning it out in the pot. Wash out in a small quantity of clean cleaner, then wipe and rub on to a clean cloth which has been moistened with solvent.

FEEDBACK AND IMPROVEMENTS

Given that the canoe is successfully completed and in use for a testing six month season, then quite soon the characteristics of the boat will begin to show. Some of these will be quite unforeseen, but the more experienced you become then the less likely are you to find freak behaviour in the canoe. People like Jorgen Samson have accurate tests made in test tanks, and thus can prove their designs before the expense of tooling up for international production. But this chapter is written for the above-average canoeist who wants to develop his interest in boats. You can recognise this *designer quality* in a canoeist when he says, and keeps on saying, 'It will *not* do'. Next is when he goes broody, and criticizes everything. Really the condition is rather depressing. Then he starts to become quite irritable, and frustration spills over into action. The first three or four attempts may not reach a conclusion, but slowly the ways reveal themselves. Eventually you have a finished boat, and everyone will delight in criticizing it. Let them. You *did* it. Listen to the criticism, reject the frivolous—but remember that you are assessing their frivolity from a committed viewpoint. Then work on the results.

    Recently I added up the number of designs which I had done. There are two main types of design: the adjusted boat, or 'pinch', is easiest, then the purely new design. Some pinches are from one's own design, or with the approval of the manufacturer, and are really adjustments of existing designs. My own scoring rate which goes back to 1962 is as follows:

Adjusted 'pinch'   3
Own design adjustment   5
Original design   8   Total   16
                   Successful boats   7

At present, as I write, there is a great anarchy in 'design adjustment'. One may copyright the design, or patent the exact lines of the boat. This is expensive, and in order to avoid legal entanglements a pirate merely needs to change the design in one small detail and the danger is averted. However, whilst pinching seems reasonable if one is setting up a school, or scout group fleet (it is still immoral of course), it is completely unjustified if one starts to make money from it by selling on a backyard industry basis.

ADJUSTMENTS

Here follow several common ways in which adjustments may be made to designs which just failed to achieve perfection. The adjusted designs won't be perfect either, but, perhaps, one day . . . This is the thing that keeps us designers going.

1. COCKPIT. SEAT TOO HIGH, OR WRONG SHAPE SEAT PAN.
   Cast new seat pan from shape required.
   Cast original cockpit rim, complete with hip side flanges.
   Place rim and hip flange piece in cockpit hole in canoe.
   Place seat pan in canoe, adjusting for side tilt, endways tile and centralization.
   Clamp with 3-inch junior clamps. Mark flanges with felt pen.
   Take out of cockpit hole. Re-clamp on bench to marks.
   Take four pieces alloy sheet, 1 inch by 3 inches, drill and screw with self-tapping screws. One screw in seat pan, two screws into hip flanges. Unscrew, unclamp, and cut flanges to butt together when screwed together again. Screw heads above alloy slips, screw threads into grp sides and seat.
   When rescrewed, try for fit in cockpit. Remove, adjust.
   When certain, two layers of grp $1\frac{1}{2}$-ounce mat behind flanges.
   When hard, remove screws, disc sharp edges off, fill to profile.
   Polish as for plug, take off moulds, make new seat.

2. COCKPIT RIM WRONG SHAPE

Make canoe from moulds, but do not fit cockpit.

Make section of the deck area surrounding cockpit required.

(Typical 'pinch') Polish deck area on required 'pinch'. Make fences fore and aft of the cockpit rim using plasticene, or even modelling clay, or possibly a shaped alloy 'fence'. Cast one half of mould.

Remove temporary fence, make other half of deck mould. Deck mould around the cockpit should be about 5 inches wide all round.

Remove when hard, bolt or clamp flanges together, cast new deck area incorporating required cockpit hole.

Copy cockpit rim and seat required. Make mould in boat —this is always difficult to remove as the seat 'in situ' is inflexible.

Lay deck area over required canoe deck. Trim it roughly to smooth profile. Replace on required deck, and mark all round with a felt pen.

Cut out required deck, and inlay new cockpit hole as neatly as possible.

Fix with four alloy slips as before.

Hang canoe upside down in slings at head height.

Place pre-wetted pieces of 1-ounce glass cloth across the gap inside.

Overlay the cloth with mat to stiffen up the link.

When hard, remove from slings, place on trestle, remove alloy slips, fill and polish. Build new moulds using existing moulds or temporary fence for flange.

3. SHRINKING A CANOE

Take the full-size mould. Using masking tape, mark out panels on the mould to be used for the canoe.

Typically, an inch off the gunwale line on the hull, about 14 inches out of the length at the maximum beam point, and 2 inches out of the centre line of the hull and deck, will produce a junior boat.

Cover the spaces between the marked out areas with polythene sheet. Cast, without gelcoat, a 3-ounce laminate on to the marked out areas.

Pull out eight pieces: forehull, right and left; rear hull, right and left; foredeck, right and left; rear deck, right and left.

Make the new forehull from two pieces, link with masking tape, lay in mould in order to get the bottom shape nearly right.

Make rear hull and fore and rear deck parts in the same way.

Link fore and rear hull on bench, using a straight edge for keel linearity, and block for rocker. Link in the middle with a number of closely spaced alloy slips and self-tapping screws. Check and re-check the line-up and rocker.

Join in the middle inside. Remove screws when hard.

Line up foredeck from nose backwards. Tape gunwale join together using alloy slips and screws if necessary, but careful workmanship should permit a join on sticky tape only.

Glass joint internally as in a normal joint.

Adjust rear deck to fit, and roughly cut the cockpit hole about the right area and shape, but slightly oversize. Fit rear deck to hull and glass up.

Fit required cockpit as before.

When thoroughly hardened off, grind down protruding corners.

Fill and smooth. Coat with 'Furane' as gelcoat is missing.

Use as new plug.

Some of the above methods may cause the professionals to throw up their hands in horror, but they work and that for me is what counts.

Finally

We are busy changing (ruining?) canoeing as we knew it. The many will seek to enjoy what the few had all to themselves a year or two ago. Anglers will oppose, canoeists will spoil . . . and yet very many will find a deep satisfaction. And it all begins in the workshop. You can't go canoeing without a canoe.

11

Fun and Games in Your Canoe

BRIAN SKILLING

IT may seem strange that a book largely devoted to the challenging aspects of canoeing should include a chapter whose main
theme is 'messing about'. It has been included, however, for
two reasons; first, that many canoeists, particularly in schools
and youth clubs, have to spend a large part of the time on one
stretch of water and may be in danger of becoming bored by
its familiarity, and second, the belief of the author that in-
dulging in stunts and games in a canoe can lead to a greater
understanding of the capabilities of both the canoeist and his
craft. With this in mind, the following are some ideas on which
the imaginative may base a rag regatta, which as a money-
raising spectator event is likely to be more successful than a
straight regatta, or which may be used as a way of relaxation
after a tough training session, or which can be practised simply
for fun.

Although all the activities suggested in this chapter can be
practised in standard canoes, all those concerned with club
activities in swimming pools and restricted waters should consider acquiring several mini-kayaks or baths trainers. Essentially
these are kayaks reduced in length to about eight or nine feet
with just sufficient buoyancy for the paddler, and designed to
give a high degree of manœuvrability. The first design of this
type to reach a wide audience was Dick Gays' 'Water flea'
which we introduced to the readers of *Canoeing* in 1966, with
the forecast that it would bring 'a new concept to indoor
canoeing'. This prophecy has proved true. The use of baths
trainers will allow more canoes afloat at the same time, enable
canoeing skills to be more quickly learnt, and will be more fun in
a restricted space. They are also a useful building exercise in
glass fibre.

THE WIGGLE AND WRIGGLE TESTS

These two tests were originally designed by the slalom canoeists to enable them to develop their boat control on still water, and to retain a measure of progress by paddling against the clock. The equipment needed is simple and can be erected on any slow moving stretch of water or in a swimming pool. A number of clubs run the 'Wiggle and Wriggle test' on a seasonal basis using a 'ladder' chart to show progress and awarding a prize at the end of the season for the paddler at the top of the ladder, and a second prize for the canoeist who has climbed the most steps of the ladder during the season.

The 'Wiggle and Wriggle' tests were first published in a magazine called *White Water*, and the following is an extract of the original article:

We have designed a standard series of manœuvres to be carried out on a standard slalom gate on standard water conditions. For the first time, therefore, we are able to compare the performance of a canoeist in Perth, Scotland with that in Perth, Australia. Not only that, we can compare the ability of a canoeist today and in ten years' time. This we feel is by far the most important thing. It enables any would-be slalomist to check how his boat handling is effected by his training techniques. It can be used to compare boats, paddles and so on. It can, alas, tell you when you are passing your peak.

It also, we hope, will give some stimulus to gate practice, for, from our own experience, we know that there is an ample enthusiasm for rough water work, but gate practice is usually thought of as a necessary evil of slalom. After great deliberation we have kept the tests as simple as possible.

We have stuck to a single gate, wide enough to cope with canadian canoes as well as folding and rigid kayaks. The test must be 'clean', that is, no poles should be touched at all. Beginners may find it useful, however, to be allowed to add penalties according to the slalom rules. This will give them a measure of progress. The first test, the 'Wiggle', can be carried out by any canoeist. The second, advanced, test is called the 'Wriggle', the extra 'r' denoting rolling. This is for the advanced slalomist, and calls for four eskimo rolls, just prior to passing through the gate at specified points. This not only means fast rolling, but also fast appreciation of the position when the roll is complete.

The test must be carried out PRECISELY as laid down.

The Gate Itself

This consists of two poles suspended by line from two screw eyes in a horizontal spacer bar. The screw eyes should be 48 inches plus the thickness of the pole apart, thus making the space between the poles exactly 48 inches. The poles should be attached to the lines in such a manner that the poles can hang vertically. The poles should be hung so that their lower ends are two inches above the water. The tests must be carried out on still water.

The Test

The run must be clean. That is, the poles must not be touched by canoe, paddle, or body. The canoeist should take up position about a boat's length from the gate. Timing starts as the bow enters the gate for the first time, and ends 'nine gates later' as the bow leaves the gate—the ninth gate being a reverse gate. The sequence MUST be adhered to, and is as follows:

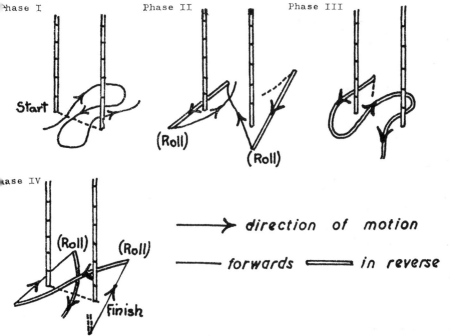

Fig. 53

Forward, Gate 1, then turn to starboard and come back through for forward, Gate 2, then turn to port and go through for forward, Gate 3. This is shown diagrammatically as 'Phase 1' (Fig. 53). You now reverse past and to the right of the gate, then do forward, Gate 4. Now reverse past and to the left of the gate, then do forward, Gate 5. This is represented in 'Phase II'. The rest of the gates are now reverse gates. Once again reverse past and to the left of the gate, then turning anti-clockwise, do reverse Gate 6R, then turning clockwise, do Gate reverse 7R. This completes 'Phase III'. The final phase, 'Phase IV' completes the test as follows. Go forward past, and to the right of the gate, then do reverse Gate 8R. When clear of the gate, go forward past and to the left of the gate, then do reverse Gate 9R. The test ends as the bow clears the gate.

The Wriggle
This is as for the Wiggle except that four rolls have been introduced. The direction and technique of rolling is not specified, but the rolls must be through 360 degrees, i.e. down one side, up the other. All rolls must take place just before tackling a gate, certainly no sooner than the 'points' shown in the diagrammatic 'course'.

CANOE POLO

Rules for Competition
1. Area of play. Any shape and size of water, but goals will face each other and be between 20 metres and 30 metres apart. Goals will consist of a metre square supported vertically with the lower edge 2 metres above the water surface. 'Out of play' areas will be defined on each pitch.
2. Ball, size 5 plastic football 27–28 inches circumference.
3. Number of players, five each side. Substitutes are only allowed for injury, and may not assist the players.
4. Two referees, and one time keeper—the time keeper to keep the score and blow for half time and full time.
5. Boats. Length—not less than 2 metres and not more than 3 metres. Beam—not less than 50 cm and not more than 60 cm. Ends—Plan—a curve at any point not less than 10 cm radius. Profile—A curve at any point not less than 5 cm radius. Buoyancy—at least 22 lb. (10 kg.) must be fitted.

6. Propulsion by paddle or hand, single bladed or double bladed.

7. Wooden blades which must not be metal tipped, and no part of the blade may have a radius of less than 3 cm in plan. Padding on metal tips is not allowed.

8. Play will be not more than seven and not less than four minutes each way. Injury time will be allowed.

9. Tie. In this event, decision will be reached by taking the following steps in order:—

   a. A one minute interval and change of ends followed by play to the first goal with no break.

   In the event of insufficient time to obtain a goal—

   b. Goal average.

   c. Goals conceded.

   d. Toss up

        (it is hoped that this should never be necessary).

10. Players will wear team bibs or some easily identified team marking.

11. *a.* Players will wear suitable helmets.

    b. Buoyancy aids or padded or pneumatic belts which afford protection to the lower lumbar region must be worn.

12. All teams must be ready to enter the water as the referee requests.

13. At the commencement of play, players will line up with their sterns on their own goal line. The ball will be placed in the middle of the playing area. Play commences when the whistle is blown.

14. At the commencement of play, after half time, and after a goal is scored, the positions described above will be taken.

15. *a.* When the ball is put out of play over the side-line the non-offending team throws it in from the point of exit, but may not throw it in the direction of attack.

    b. When the ball is put out of play over a goal line by an attacker, the defending team has a goal throw from under the goal-board. When the ball is put out of play over a goal line by a defender, the attacking team has a corner throw.

    c. No goal can be scored from a penalty throw, goal throw or corner before the ball touches some other object.

    d. For any of the above throws there must be a space of at least three metres between the thrower and his nearest opponent.

16. *a.* The paddle may be used for propulsion of the canoe,

to stop the ball in the air or to draw the ball on the surface of the water. It may not be used to strike the ball either in the air or on the water.

> *b.* Deliberate misuse or dangerous use of the paddles will be severely penalized.

17. If a player leaves his canoe he will be out of play until he is properly back in his canoe again.

18. If a player goes out of the playing area he will be out of play until he returns to the area completely with no part of his craft over the boundary line.

19. A player may tackle only the man with the ball. When the player has lost the ball the tackle must cease.

20. Obstructive play, removal of spray deck, attempts at sinking or holding under or any other form of play judged to be dangerous or unwanted will be penalized.

21. A player must dispose of the ball within three seconds of having received it, whilst it is in play.

22. Penalties will be at the discretion of the referee, these being as follows:—

> *a.* Free-throw to other side (see 15 *c* and *d*).
> *b.* Player sent off for two minutes.
> *c.* Player sent off for rest of match.
> *d.* Player referred to Polo Committee for decision.

(*Approved by the B.C.U. Canoe Polo Sub-Committee, February* 1972).

HAND PADDLING RACE

As its name implies, in this race paddlers leave their paddles behind and propel themselves by means of their hands. This is best achieved by dipping both hands in the water at the same time, leaning well forward to make the longest possible stroke. Alternatives are to equip each paddler with two plates, mugs, table tennis bats, or some similar objects. Do not make the course too long as progress is rather slow. Hand paddling races can also be held with the canoes being propelled backwards which gives greater speed but requires more skill in steering.

A variation is to scatter the water about fifty yards away from the paddlers with the appropriate number of touring paddles (one for each boat) split into their two parts. Competitors must then hand paddle up to the floating paddles, find a matching pair and then return by conventional paddling to the starting point. First home is the winner.

BROOM RACE

Each paddler is given two brooms and a length of cord or rope. The object is to lash the two brooms together so that there is a bristled head at each end and then, using this as substitute paddle, the canoeist can propel himself over the designated course.

Alternatives are to give each competitor just one broom and let them paddle their kayaks using the broom as a single blade paddle. Or, to give the competitors their brooms already lashed and treat the event as a straightforward race.

BACKWARDS RACE

Start with the sterns pointing along the course and have a simple straightline race with the canoeists paddling backwards. If there is enough room, race over a triangular course, thus requiring the paddlers to turn the canoes—but in this case make certain that the first turn is sufficiently far away to enable the competitors to string out, otherwise too much bunching on the turns may result in damage to the canoes. A variation is to require the competitors to paddle the first half of a straight course paddling conventionally, and then to paddle backwards to the starting line, which is now the finish.

SITTING ON THE STERN RACE

Paddlers sit astride the stern decks of their canoes with their feet in the water. In this position the bows will be high out of the water and the course of the canoes likely to be erratic. See that all paddlers are equally far back on the decks of their canoes and thus under the same handicap, moving forward during the race disqualifies. The race should be over a fairly short course.

STANDING RACE

Competitors propel their canoes from a standing position with feet inside the cockpit. Check that all paddles are about the same length, check also that the construction of competing canoes is suitable for this event particularly if soft-skinned boats are being used.

SINGLE-BLADED KAYAK RACE

Standard double-bladed paddles are used for this event, but competitors may only paddle on one side of the canoe, i.e. they must propel their boats using Canadian canoe techniques. The choice of paddling side may be left to each competitor. If the paddlers are reasonably competent at propelling their canoes in this fashion, a more challenging variation is to require them to cover half the course paddling only on the left hand side of their canoes, turn round a buoy, and then come back to the starting point paddling on the right-hand side of their canoes. It will be found that few kayakers can paddle with equal facility on both sides of their canoe using a single-bladed paddle stroke.

SIDEWAYS RACE

Competitors propel their canoes sideways using either a draw-stroke or a sculling stroke. The course should be a short one such as across a river or swimming bath. This event is a suitable one for a 'there and back' course which demands the use of the paddle on both sides of the canoe.

SUBMARINE RACE

Use kayaks of the slalom type with small cockpits, kneegrips, and spray covers. Competitors line up with their canoes at right angles to the course. At the starting command, they must capsize, and then *whilst remaining in the canoes* swim to the surface and using their arms swim their canoes to the finish. A very short course only is used in this event which is well suited to form part of a rolling display in a swimming pool.

CANOE RESCUE

This is a team event requiring teams of three paddlers with their canoes. On the starting signal, No. 1 of each team paddles to a given point and then capsizes. As soon as he has capsized

No. 2 and No. 3 may start off. They must paddle up to the capsized canoe, empty it out, right it and assist their team mate back into his canoe. The first team of three back to the starting point are the winners. Failure to drain the capsized canoe properly disqualifies.

A variation of this is to have team of two men only, and for the capsized canoeists to be non-competitors. In this case the capsizers take up their positions before the race and all the teams start off together.

SWIM AND RETRIEVE RACE

The canoes are taken 50 to 100 yards off shore in a lake and set adrift, or taken 50 yards upstream on a slow-moving river, and held in position by a stake boat. Competitors start from the bank, swim out to their canoes, clamber in, and paddle back to the finish.

CANOE SWAMPING CONTEST

Each canoe is equipped with a canvas or plastic bucket attached to the boat with six foot line. The object of the contest is to pour water into the other canoes until they are swamped and capsize. Touring canoes with large cockpits are best used for this. Buoyancy bags should be fitted, of course, but no spray decks.

SEEING EYE DOG RACE

For this event competitors work in teams of two, each in a single seater kayak. One member of the team is blindfolded and paddles under the direction of his sighted companion who calls out the appropriate paddling directions. The race should be over a straight course and the number of competitors should be limited so as to give each team sufficient paddling room in order to avoid collisions.

BALLOON COLLECTING CONTEST

A number of inflated balloons are released on the water some distance from the starting point. Competitors must collect as many as possible without bursting them. The winner is the paddler with the largest number of unburst balloons. When releasing the balloons attention must be paid to the wind direction.

ORGANIZING NOVELTY CANOE EVENTS AND RAG REGATTAS

The rules for novelty events must be rather flexible and will depend upon the canoes available and the type of water used. For this reason with the exception of the 'Wiggle and Wriggle Test' and 'Canoe Polo', the events outlined above have been only briefly described and are intended to provide organizers with ideas rather than rules.

The contests have been described on the assumption that single-seater kayaks will be used, since it is only in this type of craft that a paddler can learn the art of complete canoe mastery. Most of the events, of course, can be adapted for use in two-seater kayaks, or in the rare event of a club or group being able to muster sufficient Canadian canoes these could also be used. Whatever type of canoe is used, however, it is important for the organizer to check beforehand that they are in sound condition and are suited to the type of event envisaged. For example, the lightly constructed decks of the specialist long-distance racing craft should not be used for a 'Sitting on the stern race', whilst to use a standard touring canoe for the 'Wiggle' test may be challenging to the competitors it will be dull for the spectators.

This last point is important if you are organizing a fund-raising rag regatta where spectator appeal is more important than technical difficulty. Spectators will get much more excitement out of half a dozen paddlers with touring canoes racing hard in a standing position when several competitors capsize, rather than the same paddlers in narrow racing canoes moving gingerly along. Although to stand in a racing kayak may be technically more difficult.

When holding a rag regatta the organizers should plan events so that as much action as possible takes place in front of the largest part of the audience, and events should be kept sufficiently short so that attention and interest do not flag. The programme should be arranged so as to give as much variety and contrast as possible, and events where a capsize is likely should be followed by ones using different canoes, and thus avoid delay whilst canoes are brought to the shore and emptied.

In all rag regattas a rescue boat should be standing by, for although none of the events described are at all dangerous, canoeists can get into difficulties on any kind of water, and it is just possible that in the heat of competition the need for assistance may pass unnoticed unless someone is detailed to watch for such an eventuality.

The British Canoe Union Coaching Scheme—Tests and Awards

GEOFFREY SANDERS
(Chairman, B.C.U. National Coaching Committee).

AT a time of rapid growth an activity like canoeing can soon be labelled as dangerous – 'unsuitable for youngsters' – if its adherents are careless about standards of safety and performance. As the national canoeing organisation in this country, the British Canoe Union rightly felt that it had to emphasize the need for a careful and sensible approach to the sport.

With the hope of establishing standards in canoeing the B.C.U. introduced tests of proficiency as early as 1952. Since then a whole range of tests has been instituted which caters for all degrees of ability. The Elementary Canoeing Test is for the beginner who has reached a satisfactory standard after initial instruction. The certificate is often awarded at the end of short courses as an incentive for the learner to proceed to the next stage of instruction and eventually to take the Proficiency Test. The latter can be taken on inland waters in kayaks or Canadian canoes, or on the sea in kayaks. The grade could almost be likened to the motorists' driving test—the test includes what are to be considered the basic skills of the sport, and it is felt that a canoeist who passes the test should be capable of handling a canoe well under normal conditions. With the skills he has demonstrated and the application of common-sense he should prove a safe canoeist.

The Advanced Tests, on the other hand, are meant for canoeists who have had considerable experience of canoeing on difficult waters. A gold badge is awarded to those proficient enough to pass the Advanced Test for the Canadian canoe and the Advanced Inland and Sea tests for kayaks.

The Coaching Scheme developed naturally from the system of tests. As more and more people took up the sport—particularly groups from schools and youth organisations—so the need for guidance and instruction grew. Sound instruction would be vital if the progress of the sport was to be along healthy lines. The Coaching Scheme aimed to produce a large number of qualified canoeists for this important service.

A series of coaching awards was formulated in 1961 and revised in 1971. The Senior Instructor Award, taken for Inland canoeing (kayak or Canadian) or Sea (kayak only) is the basic award for group instruction and is recognized by the Department of Education and Science as the minimum requirement for teachers and youth leaders. Candidates must have passed the appropriate Proficiency Test before attending a two day approved training course, after which they will normally be appointed 'Assistant Instructors'. The two day examination for Senior Instructor is then taken some six to twelve months later. Senior Instructors can make their awards more valuable by gaining additional qualifications—by attendance at 'endorsement courses' on specific aspects of canoeing (e.g. teaching or rolling, white-water expedition work, surfing) or by taking additional Proficiency Tests and Specialist Awards (in paddle racing, slalom).

The Coach Award is intended for the experienced enthusiast who requires a good general award—for club coaches, staff in outdoor activity centres and leaders of well established canoeing groups in schools and youth groups. Such a coach needs to be qualified for sea as well as inland canoeing; candidates for the award are therefore required to hold the Advanced Sea Test and either an Advanced Inland Test or a Specialist Coach award.

As the number of canoeists with coaching awards increased it proved possible to provide a coaching service. The B.C.U. National Coaching Committee is responsible for the scheme, which is managed by a Director of Coaching, assisted by a number of part-time National Coaches. The country is divided up into Coaching areas, which roughly coincide with the sports Council regions. Each area has an Area Coaching Organiser and a number of Local Coaching Organisers to look after the interests of the counties within the area. Coaching panels, consisting of all members of the Coaching Scheme within a locality, discuss mutual problems and arrange courses and assessment sessions as required.

International Canoe Federation Members

CANOEISTS living or touring overseas can always obtain the latest information on local canoeing from the appropriate national canoeing organization. The list given below is of national canoeing organizations affiliated to the International Canoe Federation.

Argentina	Federation Argentina de Sanoas, c/o Mr Cesar E. Tardieu, Sarmiento 643–6e, Buenos Aires.
Austria	Osterreichischer Paddelsportverband, Berggasse 16, A–1090 Vienna IX.
Australia	Australian Canoe Federation, c/o Phil Coles, 8 Glasgow Avenue, Bondi Beach, 2026.
Belgium	Fédération Belge de Canoe, Secretariat National, A. Vandeput, Geerdegemvaart 79, B–2800 Mechelen.
Bolivia	Federacion Boliviana de Canotaje y Remo, P.O. Box 2951, Colon Nr. 660, La Paz.
Bulgaria	Federation Bulgare de Canoe, Bulevar Tolboukhine 18, Sofia.
Canada	Canadian Canoe Association, 333 River Road, Place Vanier, 11th Floor, Vanier City (Ottawa), Ontario, K1L 8B9.
Cuba	Federacion Cubana de Canoas, INDER, ciudad Deportiva, Via Blanco y Rancho Boyeros, La Habana.
Czechoslovakia	Czechoslovak Canoe Federation, Na porici 12, Praha 1.
Denmark	Dansk Kano og Kajak Forbund, c/o Allan Jonson, Lyngvej 26 IV, 2800 Lyngby.
Finland	Suomen Kanoottiliitto, Box 25202, Helsinki 25.

France	Fédération Française de Canoe-Kayak, 22 Avenue Victoria, Paris 1.
Germany— Federal Republic	Deutscher Kanu-Verband, Berta-Allee 8, D–41 Duisburg.
Germany— Democratic Republic	Deutscher Kanusport-Verband, Storkower Strasse 118, 1055 Berlin NO. 18.
Great Britain	British Canoe Union, 26–29 Park Crescent, London W1N 4DT.
Hungary	Magyar Kayak-Kenu Szovetseeg, Rosenberg Hazaspar u. 1, Budapest V.
Iran	Iranian Rowing and Yachting Federation, P.O. Box 1642, Teheran.
Ireland	Irish Canoe Union, c/o B. Coffey, Hillside, Kilcullen, Co. Kildare.
Italy	Federazione Italiana Canottaggio, Viale Tiziano 10, Rome.
Ivory Coast	Federation Ivoirienne de Pirogues et Canoe-Kayak, B.P. 5272, Treichville, Abidjan.
Japan	Japan Canoe Association, Kishi Memorial Hall, 1-1-1 Jinnan, Shibuya-ku, Tokyo.
Korea—Peoples Republic	Canoe Association of the Peoples Republic of Korea, Moonsin-Dong, Dongdawen District, Pyonhyang.
Luxembourg	Fédération Luxembourgeoise de Canoe-Kayak, 43 II Place de Liège, Luxembourg.
Mexico	Federacion Mexicana de Canotaje, Sanchez Ascona 1348, Mexico 10, D.F.
Netherlands	Nederlandsche Kanobond, Centraal Bureau, Sneeuwbalstraat 224, The Hague.
New Zealand	New Zealand Canoe Association, c/o Stanley M. Robinson, 20 Aubrey Street, New Plymouth.
Norway	Norges Kajakk Forbund, Youngstorget 1/III, Oslo.
Poland	Polski Zwiazek Kajakowy, Sienkiewicza 12 p. 433, Warsawa.
Rumania	Federation Romina de Kayak-Canoe, Str. Vasile Conta 16, Bucuresti.
South Africa	South African Canoe Association, c/o W. F. van Riet, 13 Leipold Street, Bellville.

Spain	Federacion Española de Piraguismo, Cea Bermudez 14, Dp. 10–11, Madrid.
Sweden	Svenska Kanotförbundet, Humlegardsgatan 17, S–114 46, Stockholm.
Switzerland	Schweizerischer Kanu-Verband, c/o Frau E. Kessler, Höhenstrasse 2, CH–4513 Langendorf 5 D.
USA	American Canoe Association, c/o Doris C. Cousin, 400 Eastern Street, New Haven, Connecticut.
USSR	Canoe Federation of the USSR, Skatertny perelok 4, Moscow 69.
Yugoslavia	Kajakaski Savez Jugoslavije, Boulevar Revolucije 44 I, Belgrade.

The Canoeist's Bookshelf

THE following list of books has been compiled from the recommendations of our contributors who were asked to suggest titles which they had found interesting or useful to them as canoeists. Books marked 'o.p.' are no longer currently available, but can probably be obtained from public libraries.

ADNEY, E. and CHAPELLE, H.
The bark canoes and skin boats of North America. United States National Museum, Bulletin No. 230, 1964.
A profusely illustrated anthropological study of the canoe in N. America.

AMERICAN RED CROSS
Canoeing. American Red Cross. 1956.
The best and most comprehensive book on single-bladed paddling, but also of value to the kayak paddler.

BLANDFORD, Percy W.
Canoes and canoeing. Lutterworth. 1962.
A good introduction with the emphasis on canoe building.

BLISS, William
Canoeing. Methuen. 1934. o.p.
A classic guide to the waterways of England and Wales based on the author's extensive cruises.

BLISS, William
Rapid rivers. Witherby. 1935. o.p.
Really talented writing about some of the most glorious canoeing rivers in Britain.

BRITISH CANOE UNION
Handbooks: 1. *Choosing your canoe and its equipment.*
2. *Canoe handling and management.*
2. *Canoe camping.*
4a. *The kayak roll.*
4b. *The Canadian roll.*

BRITISH CANOE UNION – Handbooks – *cont.*
>   5. *Canadian canoeing.*
>   6. *Long distance racing.*
>   7a. *Canoe building; soft skin and moulded veneer canoes.*
>   7b. *Canoe building: glass fibre.*

These offer a convenient and efficient way of answering the sort of questions that beginners and experts alike ask. Under continuous revision.

BRITISH CANOE UNION
>   *Coaching handbook.* Edited by G. Sanders. 4th ed. 1972.
>   Invaluable to all teaching canoeing with articles on safety, instructional techniques, meet leadership, sea coaching, swimming pool training, etc.

BRITISH CANOE UNION
>   *Guide to the waterways of the British Isles.* British Canoe Union. 3rd ed. 1961.
>   Essential for planning canoe journeys in this country.

BYDE, Alan W.
>   *Living canoeing,* A. & C. Black, 2nd ed. 1972.
>   One man's view of the sport. A stimulating book which is likely to be best appreciated by those with some knowledge of the sport.

CHAPMAN, F. Spencer
>   *Watkins' last expedition.* Chatto. 1960. Also other editions.
>   An account of Gino Watkins' fateful expedition to Greenland.

CORPS OF CANOE LIFEGUARDS
>   *The canoe lifeguard manual,* (from Mrs. C. Allan, 7 Cornwall Terrace, Penzance).
>   Contains much valuable information with an appeal far beyond members of the Corps.

HORNELL, James
>   *Water transport: origins and early evolution.* David and Charles. 1970. Reprint. A fascinating and comprehensive account of small-boat development all over the world.

MacGREGOR, John
>   *A thousand miles in the Rob Roy canoe on the rivers and lakes of Europe.* 13th ed. reprinted. British Canoe Union and Canoeing Publications. 1963.

Originally published in 1866, this is the book which founded the sport of canoeing and is still one of the best cruise narratives.

MURRAY, Al
Modern weight training. Kaye, 1963.
An excellent book covering all aspects of weight training including isometric muscle work.

PATTERSON, R. M.
The dangerous river. Allen and Unwin. 1954. o.p.
A vivid and stirring account of canoeing and trapping in the North West Territories of Canada.

PHILLIPS, C. E. Lucas
Cockleshell heroes. Heinemann. 1956. o.p.
An epic of canoeing in wartime culminating in the raid on Bordeaux harbour.

RAVEN-HART, R.
Canoe errant. Murray. 1935. o.p.
The author has probably travelled more widely by canoe than anyone before or since. This book covers some of his European travels; there are others describing his voyages in America, Africa, Asia, and Australia.

SANDERS, G.
Canoeing for schools. B.C.U., 2nd ed. 1970

SCOTT, J. M.
Gino Watkins. Hodder and Stoughton. 1935.
A study of a man who learnt to live by his kayak in Greenland.

STATE, Oscar
Weight training for athletics. Amateur Athletic Association. 1960.
A clear and concise book which although giving exercises for athletic events can be adapted to suit the needs of canoeists.

SUTHERLAND, Charles
Modern canoeing. Faber. 1964.
A refreshing book on canoeing which, while comprehensive in routine detail, puts the human side into the centre of the picture and shares the whole wide experience of canoeing with his reader.

VAN TIL, William
> *The Danube flows through Fascism.* Scribner. 1938. o.p.
>> A 900-mile voyage by two Americans down the Danube in a folding canoe. The book captures the charm and interest of leisurely canoeing down a civilized waterway.

WATTS, Alan
> *Instant weather forecasting.* Coles, 1968.
>> A useful basic book for the outdoor enthusiast.

WHITNEY, Peter D.
> *White water sport.* Ronald Press. 1960.
>> An American book which is considered to be one of the best presentations of white water canoe sport.

Notes on the Contributors

Alex and Clare Allan acquired their interest in canoeing as Instructors at the Outward Bound School, Devon. Both are B.C.U. Coaches and Chief Lifeguards of the Corps of Canoe Lifeguards. They are founder members of the Penzance Canoe Club, now regarded as the leading surf canoeing club in the country. Living in West Cornwall they are able to surf all the year round. They compete regularly in the National Surf Canoeing Championships at Bude, but also attend occasional white water and long distance events. Their two children, Gail and John, have had their own mini-canoes from an early age and were seen surfing in them on TV at the ages of 6 and 7 respectively.

Geoff Blackford is Head of the Canoeing Department of the Calshot Activities Centre. He took up rowing at school and was one of the youngest sculling champions of the Worcester Rowing Club. An ankle broken while playing tennis forced him to give up rowing, and so he joined the Worcester Canoe Club. There he became keenly interested in long-distance racing and helped pioneer this side of the sport within the club. In 1959 he won a place in the Sella River race team. After a spell of teaching in a technical college, he moved to the National Mountaineering Centre at Plas-y-Brenin were he stayed until 1965 when he took up his present post.

Alan Byde is the warden of a canoeing centre in Oxford, but claims to still think as a Northern man. Author of *Living Canoeing*, *Introduction to Canoeing for Beginners*, and *Introduction to Canoe and Coracle Building for Beginners*, also the designer of the 'Bat' range of small baths canoes and canoe polo boats. Has a reputation for unorthodoxy, but as he says, 'If it were necessary to know everything before attempting anything, nothing would get done'. Alan Byde hopes he is regarded as a man who gets things done. His canoeing activities have ranged from slalom to racing, both sprint and L.D. events, mostly at local level, and he will try his hand at anything involving canoes. He is an honorary Senior Coach of the British Canoe Union.

Oliver Cock is the Director of Coaching for the B.C.U. to which post he was raised in 1971. Previously he had been the National Coach, a post he had held since 1961. As a full-time paid official of the B.C.U. whilst he had previously spent his time touring the country organising courses and liaising with various national bodies, he is now devoting himself to the proper organization of the whole of the coaching in canoeing. He still tours and runs courses, but the organizational work is now the primary task. He has been the Coach to the British Slalom Team, and coached Paul Farrant to winning the Gold Medal in the 1959 World Championships at Geneva. He is the author of *You and Your Canoe* (1956) and with others has compiled and edited the B.C.U. instructional booklets. He has also made a number of canoe travelogue and instructional films. He take a very personal interest in the Corps of Canoe Lifeguards.

Chris Hare is a British Canoe Union National Coach in his spare time, and during the day he is a linotype operator on a daily newspaper. He has been canoeing for some twenty years and has competed in Slalom, long distance, and sprint racing, but his major interest is sea canoeing. The high point of his sea canoeing experience came when he was invited to join the British Expedition to Ubekend Ejland, West Greenland, (1966), as the kayak member. He strongly believes that the last great area of exploration by kayak is the sea and spends as much of his time doing this—and teaching others to do so.

Ken Langford is a physical education teacher at a school in Otley, Yorkshire. A member of Manchester Canoe Club since 1960, he has represented Great Britain on more than thirty occasions. He was British Slalom Champion in 1968, and a member of the British Kayak Team which gained the Silver Medal in the 1969 World Championships. He is a B.C.U. Coach and Slalom Coach and has trained canoeists not only in this country but also overseas. In the first two months of 1972 he made a coaching tour in Australia of all the states interested in slalom, winning the Australian Open Slalom Championship whilst he was there. He is a well known writer and lecturer on canoeing and outdoor activities.

Geoffrey Sanders is Deputy Headmaster at a Birmingham Grammar School, where he has been running a canoe club for over 17 years. He has been concerned with the organization of many canoe clubs, e.g. was a joint founder of the Birmingham Canoe Club, and is Founder-Chairman of the British Schools' Canoeing Association and the Birmingham Schools' Canoe Association. From 1961–5 he was the first B.C.U. Hon. Coaching Secretary and since 1965 he has been Chairman of the National Coaching Committee. A B.C.U. Council member. Editor of B.C.U. publications, *Coaching Handbook*, *Coaching Newsletter* and of the B.S.C.A. *Canoeing in Education* series. Author of *Canoeing for Schools and Youth Groups* (1966, 1970).

Brian Skilling is a chartered librarian and lecturer in communication at a college of technology. Confesses to being a dabbler, lacking the strength of purpose to pursue any branch of canoeing to its ultimate, and just enjoys casual canoeing. The founder and past editor of *Canoeing* magazine, he has also written *Basic Canoeing* (1963) and the B.C.U. pamphlet *Canadian Canoeing* (1962, 1966), and numerous articles. Thinks his contribution to the sport has been his founding of *Canoeing* magazine and his editing of this book.

Kathleen Tootill was for nineteen years a teacher in an experimental school and a director of its company. Her first outdoor love was for hockey in which she represented Manchester University and the Counties of Cheshire and Buckinghamshire. She started canoeing in 1937 on the Dorset coast. Won the Women's National Slalom Championship in 1952. Helped to pioneer river canoeing in Iceland in 1957, and in Bulgaria in 1963. Has recorded more than 8,000 miles of paddling, including 2,000 miles on the sea. Edited the *Canoe Camper* for 16 years, and is currently President of the Canoe Camping Club. She is actively involved in fighting for recognition of the necessity of British rivers for canoeists.

Marianne Wilson, formerly Marianne Tucker, international paddler for eight years, competing in the 1960 and the 1964 Olympic Games. Married to Olympic finalist Alistair Wilson, and is a director of the family business making Lendal paddles. She has been actively engaged in training people in sprint racing since 1966 when she retired from international competition having competed in two World Championship Finals. She has held all the British National Sprint and Long Distance Championship titles for women.

Index